Stained Glass
in an Afternoon®

Stained Glass
in an Afternoon®

Vicki Payne

Sterling Publishing Co., Inc.
New York

Prolific Impressions Production Staff:

Editor: Mickey Baskett
Copy: Phyllis Mueller
Graphics: Lampe Farley Communications, Inc.
Styling: Kirsten Jones
Photography: Jerry Mucklow, Pat Molnar
Administration: Jim Baskett

Library of Congress Cataloging-in-Publication Data Available
Payne, Vicki.
    Stained glass in an afternoon / Vicki Payne.
        p. cm.
    Includes index.
    ISBN 0-8069-2254-0
    1. Glass craft. 2. Glass painting and staining--Technique. I. Title

    TT298 .P38 2002
    748.5'028'2--dc21

10 9 8 7 6 5 4 3 2   2001049750

Published by Sterling Publishing Company, Inc.
387 Park Avenue South, New York, N.Y. 10016

Produced by Prolific Impressions, Inc.
160 South Candler St., Decatur, GA 30030

©2002 by Prolific Impressions, Inc.

Distributed in Canada by Sterling Publishing
c/o Canadian Manda Group, One Atlantic Avenue, Suite 105
Toronto, Ontario, Canada M6K 3E7
Distributed in Great Britain by Chrysalia Books
64 Brewery Road, London N7 9NT, England
Distributed in Australia by Capricorn Link (Australia) Pty. Ltd.
P.O. Box 704, Winsor, NSW 2756 Australia

Printed in China
All rights reserved
Sterling ISBN   0-8069-2254-0

Acknowledgements

The author wishes to thank the following companies for their generous contribution of supplies and tools for the creating of the projects in this book:

Cascade Lead Products
1614 West 75th Ave.
Vancouver, BC V6P 6G2

Cooper Tools/Weller
P.O. Box 728
Apex, NC 27502
www.coppertools.com

Vic's Crafts
8349-K Arrowridge Blvd.
Charlotte, NC 28273
www.foryourhome.com

Glastar Corporation
www.glastar.com

Plaid Enterprises, Inc.
www.plaidonline.com

Glass Accessories International

Toyo Glass Cutters

About Vicki Payne

Vicki Payne is an educational leader of the home decor and crafting industries. As CEO of Cutters Productions, she produces the nationally syndicated television shows: *Glass with Vicki Payne*, *Paint! Paint! Paint!*, and *For Your Home*, which she co-hosts with her daughter, Sloan. Together, these weekly 30-minute programs are carried by more than a 160 different public television stations and GoodLife TV on cable. In addition to hosting her own shows, Vicki is host of *D.I.Y. Crafts* on HGTV's D.I.Y. Network. She is a frequent guest on home improvement and crafting shows, including *The Carol Duvall Show*, *Home Matters*, *Kitty Bartholomew: Your Home*, and *Decorating with Style*.

Vicki has produced how-to videos for over ten years, created her own consumer glass show, *The Glass Extravaganza*, is frequently published in craft and trade magazines, and serves as a consultant to companies throughout the craft and hobby industries. She has succeeded by sharing her passion and by making her talents accessible to others.

A member of the Art Glass Suppliers Association (AGSA), Hobby International Association, Association of Creative Crafts, Designers Association, and the Society of Craft Designers, she has served on the AGSA Board of Directors and as Chairperson of the AGSA Manufacturers' Committee.

STAINED GLASS • *In an Afternoon*

Stained Glass –
Beautiful, Quick & Easy

Who hasn't admired the beauty of stained glass and marveled at the rich colors, the gorgeous textures, the sparkle of the glass, the soft gleam of metal edging? But chances are you thought stained glass wasn't something you could make—it seemed so difficult, so time-consuming. Think again!

In this book, stained glass artist Vicki Payne de-mystifies the basic techniques for copper foil stained glass and stained glass mosaics and presents more than 25 stained glass projects you can make in an afternoon.

First you'll learn how to choose supplies and tools. Then Vicki shows you, step-by-step, how easy it is to prepare, cut, assemble, apply foil, solder, frame, and finish—everything you need to know to craft your own glass projects.

You'll find instructions and patterns for making colorful panels and window ornaments, terrific tabletop accessories like frames and candle holders, and gleaming garden cloches to protect tender plants. You'll see Vicki's fail-safe, easy technique for making beautiful boxes and learn how to make marvelous glass mosaics for your home and garden.

Relax, have fun, and enjoy! That's the true beauty of stained glass.

Supplies for Getting Started

Stained Glass

*There are two basic categories of stained glass—**opalescent glass** and **cathedral glass**. Opalescent glass is glass you cannot see through. Cathedral glass is glass you can see through. Glass can come in any color or texture, whether it is opalescent or cathedral—the difference is the density. Some cathedral glass is clear, but textured.*

Glass is sold by the square foot or by the pound. A square foot of glass is usually 12" x 12". If you are buying glass by the pound, you generally get 1-1/2 pounds of glass to the square foot. It is a good rule of thumb to buy about 25% more glass than the size of your project; you may use more than you anticipated. It is always a heartbreaker to go back to the glass shop and find that there is no more of the glass you need in stock and have to wait for the next shipment to come in. Always buy more—you can save it for a future project.

You should expect to spend from $2.50 to $7.00 a square foot, depending on the color of the glass.

When choosing glass colors, the best rule of thumb is to use what you like. If you like pink, use pink. If you like yellow, select yellow. Feel free to change the colors of any of the projects in this book to suit your taste or your decor.

Glass Types & Textures

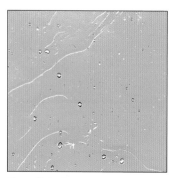

Smooth texture

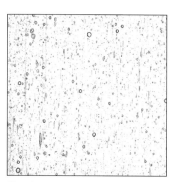

Seedy texture

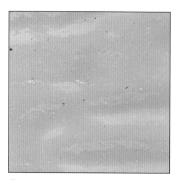

Flemish texture

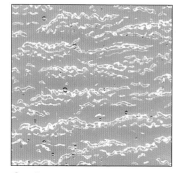

Granite texture

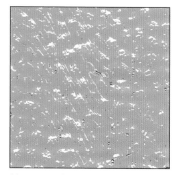

Hammered texture

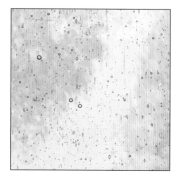

Iridized texture

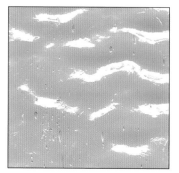

Ripple texture

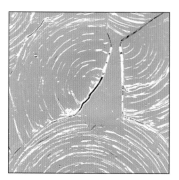

Rondolite texture

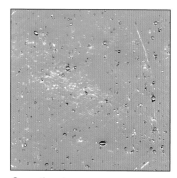

Smooth catspaw

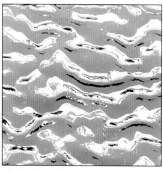

Tight ripple texture

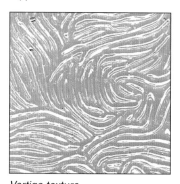

Vertigo texture

Wavolite texture

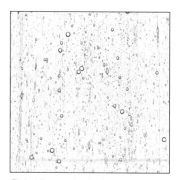

Pale blue cathedral

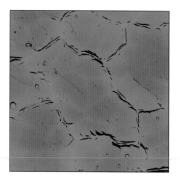

Light green cathedral

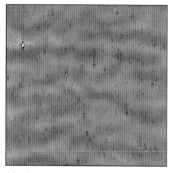

Medium purple cathedral

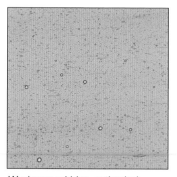

Wedgewood blue cathedral

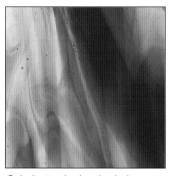
Cobalt streaked cathedral

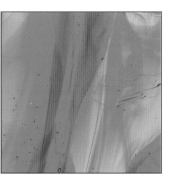
Green/clear streaked cathedral

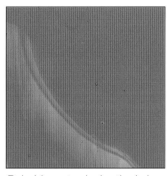
Ruby/clear streaked cathedral

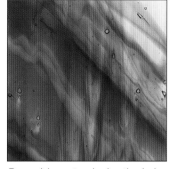
Brown/clear streaked cathedral

Clear opalescent

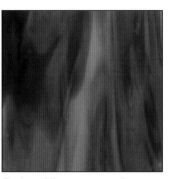
Dark and lime green opalescent

Bright yellow opalescent

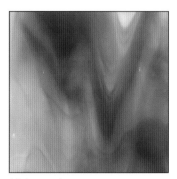
Violet opalescent

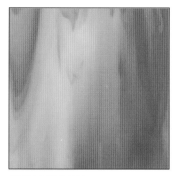
Red opalescent

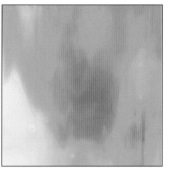
Sky blue opalescent

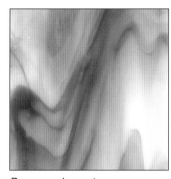
Brown opalescent

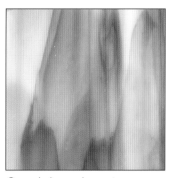
Green/ruby opalescent

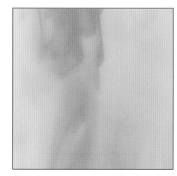
Peachy orange opalescent

Light amber opalescent

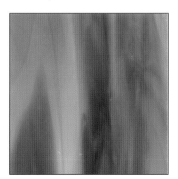
Green/blue opalescent

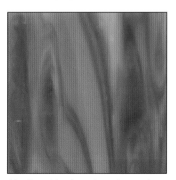
Medium blue/royal opalescent

Glass Cutting Tools

Glass cutters are the tools used to score glass so it can be cut. The score, a barely visible scratch or fissure made on the surface of the glass by the metal wheel of the cutter, weakens the glass at the site of the score and makes it easier to break.

Carbide Cutters

Handheld **carbide cutters** are the ones you'll use for most of your glass cutting. They come with different handles in a variety of styles and range in price from just a couple of dollars to about $20. The cutting wheels of all glass cutters need to be lubricated with oil, so a **self-oiling cutter** is convenient to use— it automatically lubricates the wheel as you score. Most of today's glass carbide cutters are self-oiling.

Strip Cutter

A **strip cutter** is a glass-cutting tool that can be set to a desired width. It will cut straight, parallel, uniform strips of glass again and again. It's especially useful for making boxes.

Strip-Circle Cutter

A **strip-circle cutter** is a glass cutting tool that can be set to cut both strips and circles in a range of sizes.

Lubricating Oil

Lubricating oil is necessary to protect the cutting wheel so the glass cutter will last much longer and because a score line which has been lubricated with oil is much easier to break.

Simply fill the well of the self-oiling cutter with the lubricating oil. If your cutter is not self-oiling, you'll need to saturate a towel with lubricating oil and keep it handy. Pass the wheel of the cutter over the oil-saturated towel before each score.

You can buy lubricating oil or mix your own. I like to use a mixture of equal amounts of motor oil and lamp oil.

Pictured top to bottom, right: Pistol grip cutter, Thompson grip cutter, comfort grip cutter, brass-handled cutter. At left: A strip cutter.

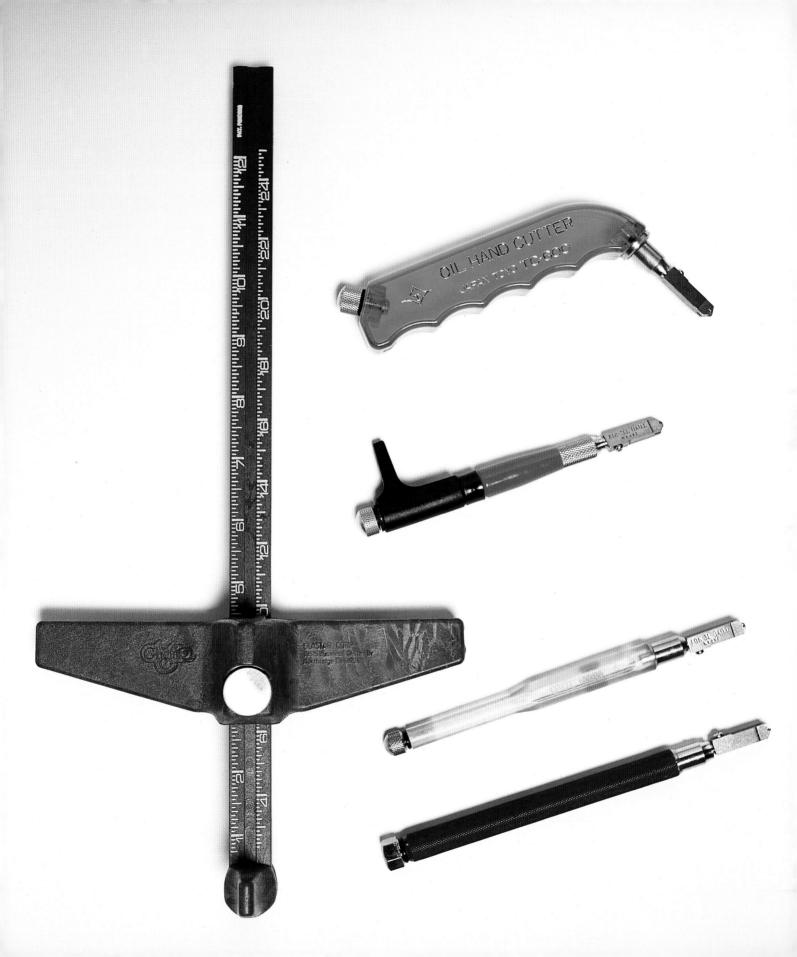

Glass Breaking Tools

Glass breaking tools can be used as extensions of your hands to hold and break glass.

Running Pliers

Running pliers have curved jaws with a raised ridge on the bottom. Use running pliers to help you push the score line through the glass so you can break it with the pliers instead of with your hands. A mark on the top jaw helps you position the pliers on the score line. Use only for straight cuts or outside curves. Never use for inside curves.

Breaking Pliers

Breaking pliers have jaws that are flat on the inside. When you need to hold a piece of glass to break it and do not have room for two hands, use these. Position the edge of the breakers parallel to the score line.

Grozing Pliers

Grozing pliers have little teeth like a file on both the top and the bottom jaws. Use these pliers to chip away at the little unwanted pieces of glass that remain along a cut after scoring and breaking.

Combination Pliers

Combination pliers have a flat jaw and a curved jaw. Both jaws are serrated. Combination pliers can be used both for breaking and grozing. Use the curved side up for grozing and the flat side up for breaking.

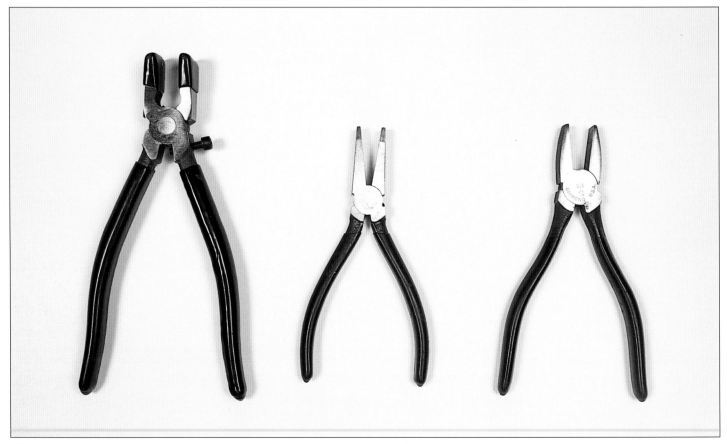

Pictured left to right: running pliers, grozing pliers, breaking pliers.

Safety Gear

Protective Glasses

Always wear **protective glasses, goggles, or a face shield** when cutting and grinding glass to shield your eyes from glass chips and fragments and splattering flux or solder.

Face Mask

When you are soldering, wear a **face mask** specially designed to protect you from soldering fumes. They are available at stained glass stores and hardware stores. **Always** work in a well-ventilated area when soldering.

Glass Smoothing Supplies

Glass smoothing supplies prepare the edges of cut glass pieces for the application of copper foil and correct minor problems in the shape of a piece of glass, ensuring that pieces will fit together as intended.

Glass Grinder

An electric **glass grinder** is a machine with a diamond bit and a tray underneath the bit that contains water. There is a sponge in the back that pumps water up to the bit to keep it wet when you are grinding. The water keeps the dust down and keeps the glass cool so it will not fracture.

A grinder is the fastest, most efficient way to prepare and correct problems on the edges of glass pieces. Grinders can cost between $70-$150. You might want to check with your local glass shop about renting one. When you use a glass grinder, always wear safety glasses and follow the manufacturer's instructions.

Emery Cloth/Carborundum Stone

An **emery cloth** or a **carborundum stone** also may be used to smooth the edges of cut glass pieces. Be forewarned that using the carborundum stone or emery cloth is a slow process, but less expensive than buying a grinder.

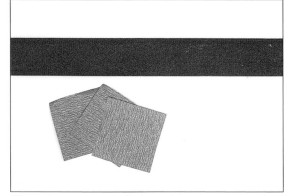

Pictured top to bottom: Carborundum stone, emery cloth.

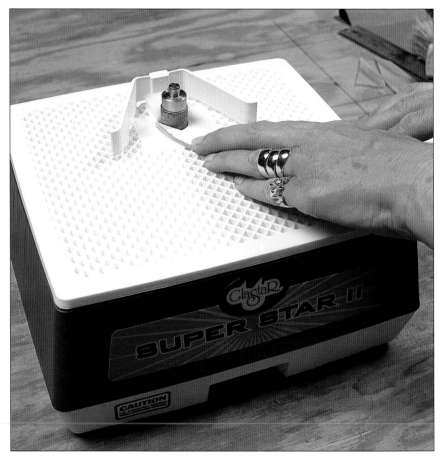

A glass grinder.

Pattern Making Supplies

When you are first starting out, it is better to use a pattern designed specifically for stained glass. When you become more experienced, you can create your own designs. Use these supplies to make patterns for cutting out glass pieces and assembling your projects.

Pattern Paper

I like to use **white bond paper or white craft paper** for patterns—white instead of brown because it is easier to see the colors of the colored pencils. (I color in the design with colored pencils to see if the colors work together.) If you use a light box for tracing the pattern lines on the glass, white paper is easier to see through.

Tracing Paper

Use **tracing paper** and a **pencil** to trace patterns from this (and other) books. Buy tracing paper at crafts and art supply stores.

Transfer Paper

Use **transfer paper** to transfer designs to pattern paper. You can also use a photocopier to make copies of traced designs. But remember that photocopiers can distort your designs, especially larger window patterns.

Colored Pencils

Cutting the pieces for your stained glass projects is easier if you take the time to color in the design with **colored pencils**. That way, you create a color-keyed pattern that's especially helpful when you cut the pattern out to make templates for cutting.

Ruler

The most important tool you need is a **metal ruler**. An 18" ruler is a good size to have. Make sure it's calibrated from one end all the way to the other. Also make sure it has a cork back. This will prevent it from slipping around while you are drawing and using it to cut glass.

Pattern Shears

Stained glass is composed of pieces of glass separated by pieces of metal or solder all the way across a project, and the metal takes up space between each piece of glass. When you cut out pattern pieces with **pattern shears** to make templates for cutting your glass, the special blades of the pattern shears (there are three of them) remove a small strip of paper on the cutting lines to allow space for the metal.

You might want to practice cutting with pattern shears on some scrap paper before you cut out your pattern to make templates.

Rubber Cement

Use **rubber cement** or a **pattern fixative** to hold pattern pieces in place for cutting and grinding. Either will simply rub off the glass when you're ready to construct your piece.

Masking Tape

You also need **masking tape** to hold your design in place on your work board and for holding pieces of glass for lampshades and boxes together until you solder them.

Markers

To mark on glass, choose markers that aren't permanent on glass and can be rubbed or washed off. Test **felt-tip markers** on a scrap of glass before using. A **china marker**, available at crafts and art supply stores in a variety of colors, is another good choice for marking glass.

Other Supplies

It is a good idea to get a **shoebox** to put your cut-apart pattern pieces in so you don't lose any of them. If you do happen to lose a pattern piece during the process of building your window, you can always make a tracing off your other (un-cut) copy.

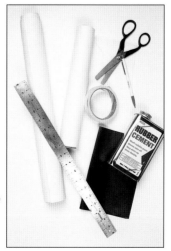

Pictured clockwise from left: Pattern paper, tracing paper, pattern shears, pencil, masking tape, rubber cement, transfer paper, ruler.

Soldering Supplies

To make stained glass panels, windows, and objects like lampshades and boxes, glass pieces are wrapped with foil tape or metal came and are joined together with solder.

Foil Tape

The foiling method is used for most of the projects in this book. **Foil tape** is wrapped around each piece of glass before soldering. One side of the tape is smooth; the other side is sticky. The sticky side goes towards the edge of your glass. Available in copper or silver, foil tape is sold in various widths. The width needed for each project is specified in the individual project instructions. Also referred to as **Copper Foil Tape.**

Burnisher

A **burnisher** or foilmate is a specialized tool with a roller on one end and a slot on the other. It is used to press the foil tape against the glass and create a tight bond.

You can also burnish foil tape with a wooden chopstick, a craft stick, an orange peeler, or a lathekin.

Craft Knife

Use a **craft knife** fitted with a #11 blade to cut copper foil tape.

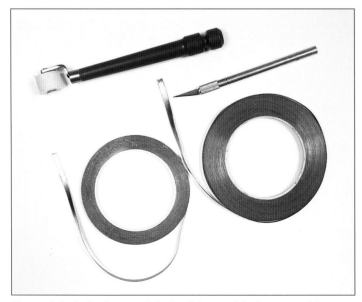

Pictured clockwise from top left: Burnisher, craft knife, copper foil tape, silver foil tape.

Flux

Flux is a cleaner that prepares metal to accept the solder. Without flux, soldering isn't possible. I recommend a water-soluble flux, which can be washed off your project with dishwashing soap and water and can be left on your project overnight or until the next day without doing damage.

When you're working, it's a good idea to pour some flux out of the container it comes in and into a wide-mouth jar. Don't ever go back and forth from the container the flux comes in to your project. You'll weaken the strength of the flux if you do.

Apply flux to your project with a **flux brush**. These brushes rust out after a while (continuing exposure to the flux corrodes them), so it's a good idea to buy a couple at a time.

Solder

Solder is the molten metal used to join the metal-wrapped glass pieces. It looks like thick wire and comes on a spool. For copper foil, you'll work with a solid-core solder labeled "60/40." The numbers indicate how much tin (60%) and lead (40%) are in the solder.

Soldering Iron with Rheostat

To solder stained glass, you need a **soldering iron**, not a soldering gun. You can't use a soldering gun on your stained glass project. The **rheostat** controls the temperature of the soldering iron. Soldering irons have tips of various sizes that come with them. For many copper foil projects, a tip 1/4" wide is used.

An **iron stand** keeps your iron from rolling around on your work surface and protects you from the hot parts of the iron when you are working.

Tip Cleaner

A **tip cleaner** is simply a sponge that is kept wet so that you can wipe off the tip of your soldering iron as you work to keep it clean and completely shiny. If you work with a soldering iron tip that is all dark, you won't be able to do a good job of soldering.

Pictured from top left: Soldering iron rheostat with iron holder, 80 watt soldering iron, flux and flux brush, solder, 100 watt thermostatically controlled soldering iron.

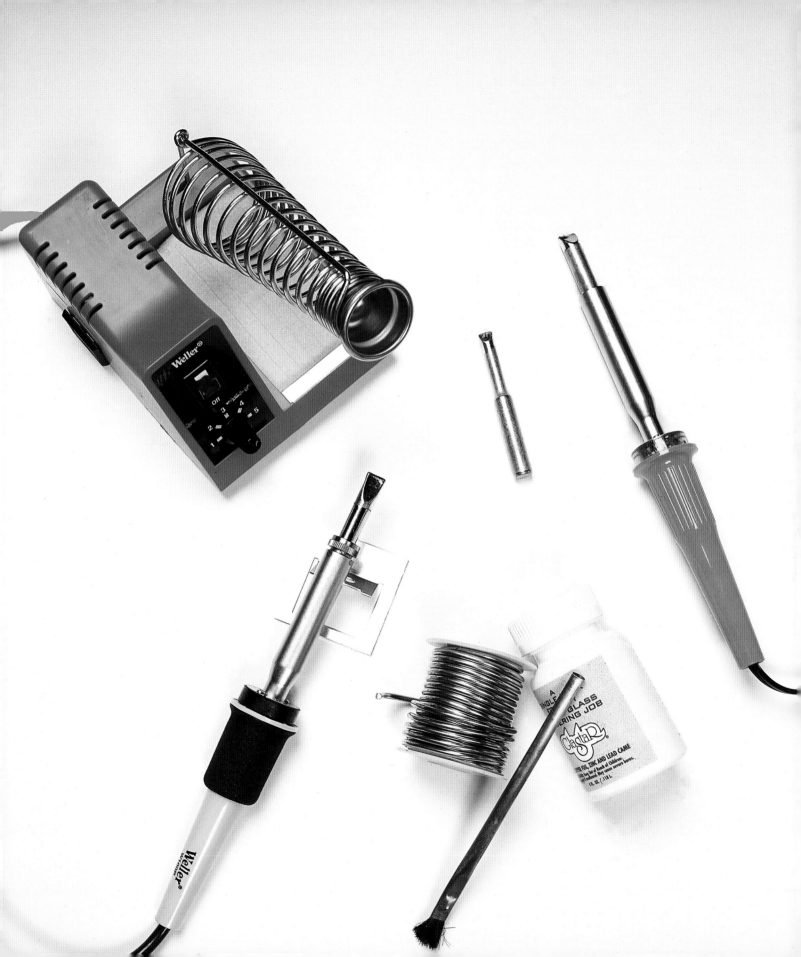

Assembling Supplies

*Choose a working area with a table at a comfortable height with enough space
to spread out your project, good light, convenient access to electrical outlets, good
ventilation, and a hard-surface floor that is easy to clean.*

Work Board

Your **work board** is the surface you'll use for cutting and assembling your glass projects. It should fit comfortably on your work table and be bigger than the project you're making. A piece of plywood 5/8" or 3/4" thick is one option. Another option is Homasote, a building material that's often used to make bulletin boards. Buy plywood and Homasote at building supply stores.

Squaring Bars

Squaring bars are used to hold the edges of projects with straight borders for assembling and soldering. You can buy metal bars made for this purpose or fashion your own with strips of wood. Hold squaring bars in place with push pins. Wooden strips could be nailed in place on a wooden work surface.

Triangle

You also need a **drafting triangle** to assist you in setting up the squaring bars. The triangle should have a 45-degree angle on one end and a 90-degree angle on another.

Desk Brush & Dust Pan

It is a good idea to have a **desk brush** and a **dust pan** handy so that periodically you can sweep away little glass chips and scraps that accumulate on your work surface. It's really easy to ruin a good piece of glass by putting it down on top of a stray chip of glass on your work surface—the chip can cause the big piece to snap.

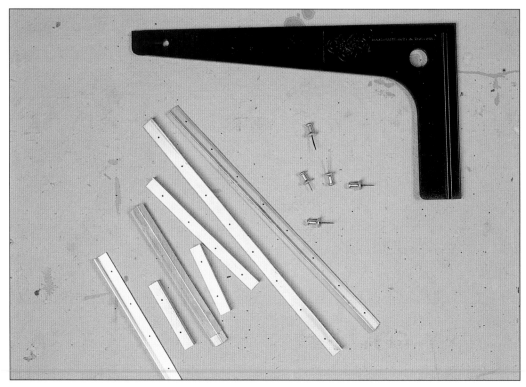

Pictured top to bottom: triangle, push pins, metal squaring bars—arranged on a work board.

Project Edging & Hanging Supplies

You need to have some sort of frame around a stained glass panel in order to keep it from bending when you display it. Ready-made or custom-made metal or wooden picture frames can be used, or you can make frames to fit your piece with U-shaped came.

U-Shaped Came

U-shaped came is used to frame stained glass panels. It is made of extruded lengths of zinc, brass, and copper and has a channel on one side that holds the glass. It is sold in 6 ft. lengths.

Came Notcher

Use a **came notcher** to cut the U-shaped came at a 45-degree angle to make neatly mitered corners for your frames.

Measure the came for notching with a **ruler**—the same one you used for pattern making and cutting. Came can also be cut with **lead nippers.**

Hanging Loops

You can make your own loops for hanging from tin-coated **12 gauge copper wire**. (You can tin the wire yourself by applying flux to the wire and coating it with solder.) Form the loops with **needlenose or roundnose pliers**, and use the pliers to hold the loops in place while you solder them to the frame of your project. Thread **monofilament fishing line** through the loops and secure it for hanging.

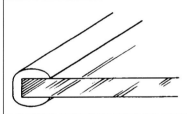

U-Shaped Came.

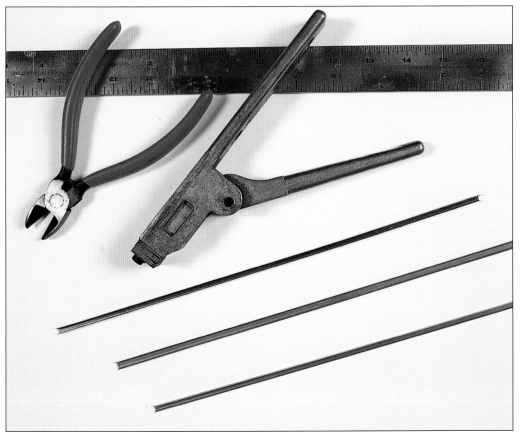

Pictured top to bottom from top left: Ruler, lead nippers, came notcher, zinc U-shaped came, brass U-shaped came, copper U-shaped came.

Glass Decorations & Finishes

A variety of materials can be used to decorate and embellish stained glass pieces. The projects in this book include examples of how to incorporate decorations in your designs.

Beveled Glass Pieces

Beveled glass pieces are clear pieces of glass with edges that have been beveled and polished. They're ready to use—no cutting is necessary. In this book, you'll see how they can be used as the main glass pieces of a project and as dimensional accents. They come in a variety of sizes and shapes, including squares, rectangles, and triangles.

Glass Nuggets

Glass nuggets are round-shaped pieces of glass with rounded tops and flat backs. Also called "flat-backed marbles" or "glass globs," glass nuggets are used to add decoration and dimension to stained glass projects. They come in a variety of sizes and colors.

Glass Jewels

Glass jewels are pressed or molded glass pieces with flat backs. They can be used for decoration, to add dimension, or to create patterns in glass designs. They come in a variety of colors and shapes.

Other Decorations

A variety of other materials can be used to decorate stained glass projects, including seashells, glass marbles, and glass beads.

Patina Finishes

Special stained glass patina finishes are available. They work by creating chemical reactions with the tin and lead of the solder and are often used to impart an aged look. Always work in a well-ventilated area and wear rubber gloves when applying patinas. Follow the manufacturer's instructions for application.

Pictured clockwise from top left: Seashells, glass nuggets, glass marbles and glass beads, glass jewels, beveled glass pieces. copper wire.

Crafting Your First Project

*In this section, you'll see how to cut out a pattern, cut glass, use a grinder,
put on copper foil, solder, and frame the finished project for display.*

How Much Glass?

For the projects in this book, the amount of glass you need to complete the project is included in the Supplies list for each project. I wanted to make that part easy because estimating how much glass you need can cause problems for even experienced glass workers. Here are some guidelines, using the Tulip Panel project that follows as an example.

For the background of the panel, which measures 12" x 8", if you bought a 12" x 12" piece of glass, you would have enough glass to cut out all of the pieces and, if necessary, enough to re-cut a couple of the pieces if you have a problem. To cut out the flower and the leaves, you are going to need about twice as much glass as the space you are filling on the panel. It would be a good idea to get twice as much pink glass as the area of the flower to give enough space to rotate the pattern pieces so the grain of the glass is going in the most attractive direction.

For this first project, the background is cream opalescent glass, and you need to buy one square foot. For the pink tulip, you need to buy one-half square foot. For the green opalescent leaves, you need another one-half square foot.

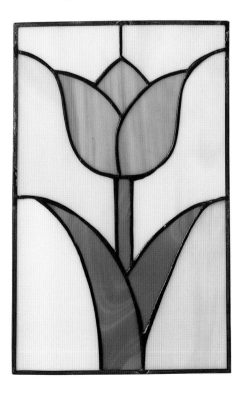

Step 1 • Prepare Your Pattern

1. Position tracing paper over the pattern and trace the design lines with a pencil. Use arrows to mark the desired direction of the grain of the glass on the pattern. You will want the grain of the glass running in the same direction, no matter the color. So you need to add grain arrows. Once the pattern pieces are cut out it is hard to determine the top from bottom, or where they are within a design. Number the pattern pieces so that they can be matched with the assembly pattern after cutting out. I also add a letter after each number to indicate pattern piece of similar color. For example "A" might be the background color; "B" could be the flower color.

2. Transfer the design to white pattern paper or photocopy the traced design. You want to have two copies of the pattern—one to cut apart to make templates for cutting the glass and another to use as a guide when assembling the piece.

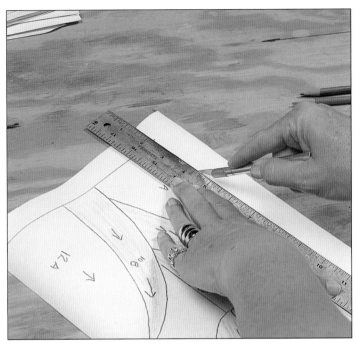

4. Cut the outside edges of pattern, using a ruler and a craft knife to get a clean, straight edge.

3. Color-code the pattern with colored pencils that correspond with glass colors you've chosen. This makes it easier to identify the pattern pieces after you've cut them apart to make the templates.

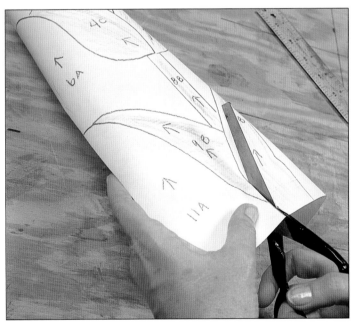

5. Use pattern shears to cut out the pattern pieces you will use as cutting templates. Put the single blade up toward you and start cutting with small strokes, not big ones. Hold your paper in your other hand and cut right along the line. Continue cutting until you have cut out every piece of your pattern. It doesn't matter the order you cut it out in; do whatever seems easiest for you.

Step 2 • Cutting Glass Pieces

Caution! Always wear safety glasses to protect your eyes when cutting glass.

2. To break the glass, pick it up and put your fingers under the glass and your thumbs on top. Rock your hands up and away from you. The glass will break along the scored line.

1. Determine how much glass you will need to cut your first piece by positioning the pattern piece on the glass. Divide the larger piece into a smaller, more manageable piece that will be enough to cut all of the pieces of that color. Score piece of glass from the larger piece, using your glass cutter.

3. Apply pattern fixative or rubber cement to backs of pattern pieces. Option: If you have a light box, you can place the pattern on the light box and position the glass over the pattern. (The pattern lines will be visible through the glass.) Use a china marker or felt-tip marker (one that's not permanent on glass) to transfer the pattern lines to the glass.

4. There is a right side and a wrong side to glass for cutting. The right side—the front—is generally smoother. The wrong side—the back—has a little bit of a bump to it. Position the pattern pieces on the right (smooth) side of glass, aligning the arrows you marked on the pattern pieces with the grain of the glass. Allow 1/4"-1/2" all around each piece to make breaking out the pieces easier.

5. This photo shows how to hold the cutting tool properly. Note the placement of the fingers and thumb and the angle of the cutting tool in relation to the glass.

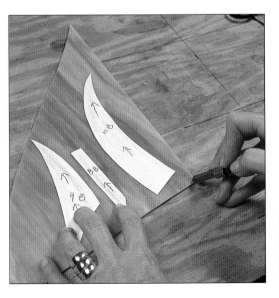

6. To begin cutting the first pattern piece, start the cut at the edge of the piece of glass and move the cutter to the edge of the pattern template.

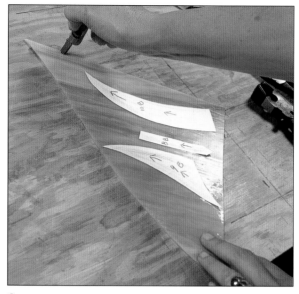

8. Finish the cut by continuing past the edge of the pattern template and off the edge of the glass.

7. Continue the cut along the edge of the pattern template.

9. Break the glass with breaking pliers, holding the glass surface in one hand and holding the pliers parallel to the score line, but not over the score line. Position the edge of the pliers on the scored line. Breaking pliers work well on curved cuts. Use the same technique to score and break the other two sides of the piece—scoring, then breaking; scoring, then breaking. Always score the inside curves first, then the outside curves. Score straight lines last.

10. Use running pliers on straight cuts, like this stem piece. Score the glass from one edge to the other along the pattern template's edge. Align the mark on the running pliers with the scored line to break the glass.

11. Use grozing pliers to break away any small chips or flanges of glass that protrude on the edges of cut pieces. You will save a lot of time if you use your grozing pliers to remove most of the unwanted glass before you go to the grinder. *TIP:* To ensure a clean work surface, periodically sweep off your work surface with a brush to remove small chips and slivers of glass that accumulate as you work.

12. To cut deep curves, make successive scores and breaks to gradually move into the final cut. The dotted lines show how this background piece could be scored and separated.

13. Smooth the edges of each cut piece with a carborundum stone or a piece of emery cloth.

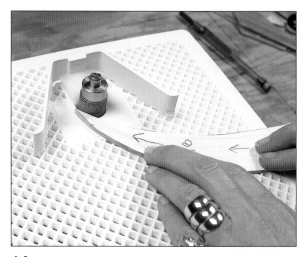

14. Or use an electric glass grinder to smooth the edges. Keep the pattern pieces attached to the glass as you work on the edges.

Step 3 • Assembling the Project

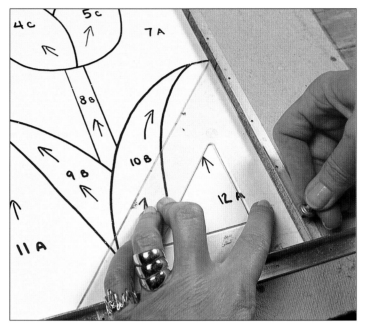

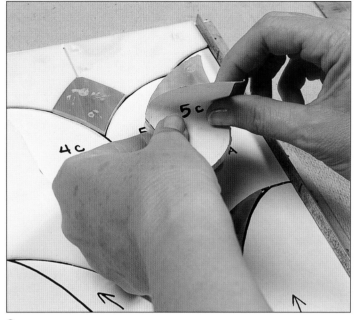

1. Set up your work space by first placing intact pattern on surface. Your glass pieces will be assembled on top of this pattern. Place the squaring bars around three sides of the intact copy of your pattern. Use a triangle to be sure the bars are perfectly square. Leave one end open for moving the pieces in and out.

2. Working one piece at a time, remove the pattern template from the cut glass piece and position the piece over the appropriate part of the pattern.

3. Continue positioning until all pieces are in place.

4. If the pieces are too tight or don't fit well, use a piece of emery cloth or an electric grinder to work on the edges and reduce the size of the piece.

5. When all pieces are fit and placed, add the last squaring bar and secure in place. Leave the pieces within the squaring bars during the foiling process, picking up only one piece at a time to apply the foil. Otherwise, the pieces might not fit together.

Step 4 • Foiling the Glass Pieces

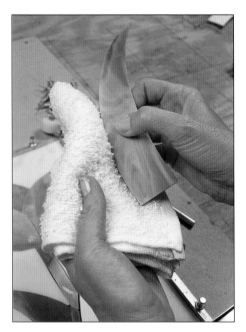

1. Wipe the edges of all the glass pieces with a cloth to remove any oil residue from the glass cutter and all the powder from the grinder or carborundum stone.

2. Pull the backing paper from the end of the roll of foil tape and position the edge of the glass piece on the foil, centering the edge of the glass piece on the tape.

3. Keep applying foil tape around the piece to cover ALL the edges of the piece. Keep the piece centered on the foil so the foil overlaps the piece equally on both sides. (This is the easiest part of doing stained glass. If you're making a big project like a lampshade, you may have to apply foil to as many as a thousand pieces—it's time consuming, but not difficult.)

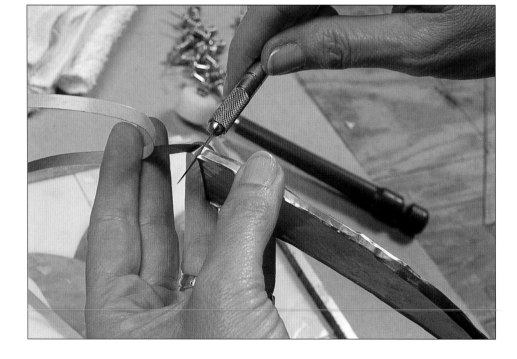

4. When all the edges of a piece have been covered and you get to the point where you started, overlap the foil tape slightly—about 1/4"—and cut the end of the foil tape with a craft knife.

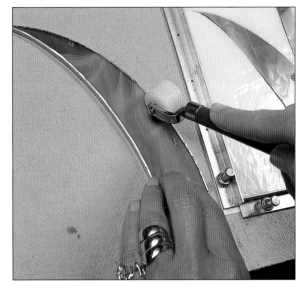

6. Burnish the tape to the sides of the glass piece to secure the foil, using the roller end of the burnisher. Be sure to burnish both sides of the glass piece. If you have done a good job, you won't be able to see where you overlapped it at the beginning and end of the foil and you won't be able to feel a ridge between the glass and the foil. It should be perfectly smooth on the edges.

5. Burnish the tape on the edge of glass for a smooth, secure bond. Run the grooved end of the burnisher around the edge of the glass to press the tape securely against the edge. **Don't** run your fingers along the edge of the glass—that's a good way to get a foil cut.

7. Continue the foiling process until foil has been applied to all pieces. Work one piece at a time, replacing the pieces within the squaring bars after you apply the foil.

Step 5 • Soldering Glass Pieces

Caution: Always solder in an area with adequate ventilation. Soldering fumes are not healthy to breathe.

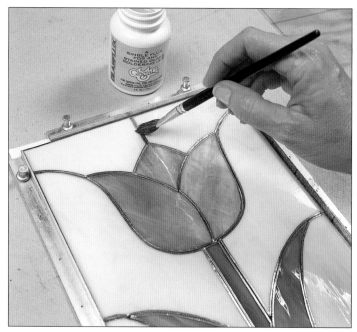

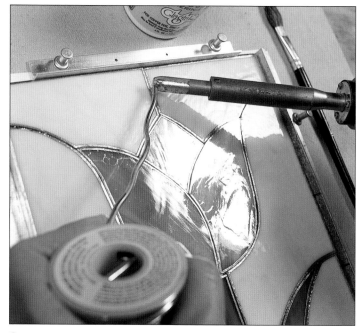

1. Heat soldering iron. Brush flux on the first area you plan to solder. You do not have to be precise. Make sure you cover the foil, but it is okay if you get some flux on the glass.

2. Position tip of soldering iron over the foiled area, holding the iron in one hand and the roll of solder in the other hand. Hold the solder wire against the iron to melt the solder as you move along.

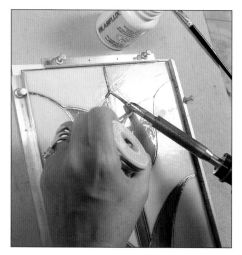

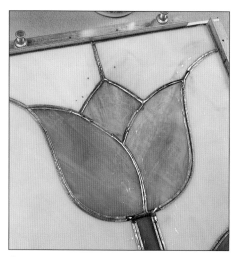

5. When you've completed one side of the piece, turn it over and solder the other side. *TIP:* If you notice drip-through on the other side when you turn it over, take a wet cloth and lay it underneath the piece as you work. That will cool the solder more quickly and stop the drip-throughs from seeping to the other side.

3. Draw the tip of the soldering iron along the flux-brushed foil, melting solder as you go. The solder will stay on the metal area and resist the glass.

4. Continue to solder, working one area at a time—first applying flux, then soldering. For a smooth bead of solder at joints where pieces intersect, run the solder a short way in each direction from the joint.

Step 6 • Framing the Piece

Panels will need to be stabilized on the edges with a frame of caming. Even if you are going to frame your piece in a wooden frame, I like to add caming around the piece to strengthen it.

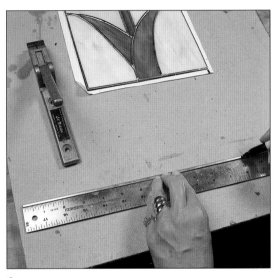

2. Mark each measurement **in order — working clockwise** on a length of U-shaped came with a felt-tip marker. The marks indicate where the came will be notched so the piece of came will fold around the edges of the panel, forming mitered corners. For example, for an 8" x 10" vertical piece — mark 8", then 10", then 8", then 10".

1. When you've finished soldering and removed the squaring bars, measure each side of the piece to determine how much U-shaped came you need to frame the panel, working clockwise. Add the measurements together for each side to get a measurement for the total length of came needed. For example, if you have an 8" x 10" panel, you will need a piece of came 36" long (8" + 8" + 10" + 10")

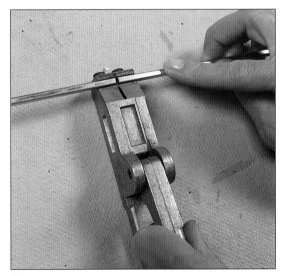

3. Notch the came at the places where you have marked, using a came notcher.

4. This closeup shows the came with a notch cut for mitering.

5. Place the U-shaped came around the panel, bending the came at the notches and positioning the notches at the corners. Use push pins to hold the came in place around the panel.

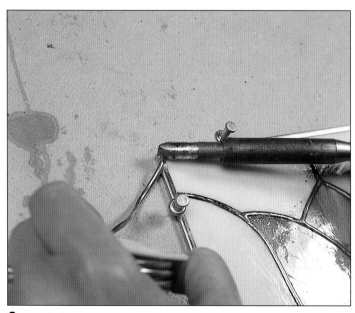

6. Brush flux on the joint where the two ends of the came come together at one corner and solder. Remember to brush flux on the joint before soldering. When you have soldered one side, turn the panel over and solder the joint on the other side.

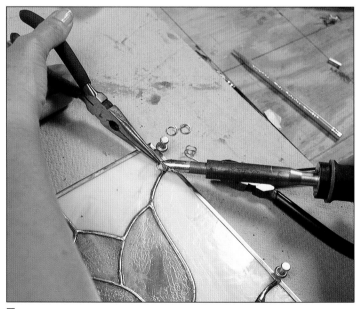

7. *Optional:* You can create little eyes of wire for hanging you panel using aluminum wire. Use roundnose pliers to form circles of wire for the hanging loops. Solder a wire circle at each side of the panel on the back. Attach monofilament line through the loops for hanging the panel.

Tips for Successful
Stained Glass

Scoring the Glass

You should score a piece of glass only once. Do not go over a score line twice—that's a good way to ruin your cutter, and your cut is not going to be successful.

Determining a Cutting Order

It's a good idea to cut the big pieces first and then the little ones. If you make a mistake you can use your scrap glass to cut out the other piece(s).

Tack-Soldering

Many times you will be instructed to "tack-solder" a project. Tack-soldering holds pieces together so they won't move as you create your solder seams.

To tack-solder, dab a small amount of flux at any point along a foil seam. Touch the solder and the hot iron to the flux for a very short time—about a second—to create a dab of molten solder. When the solder cools, it will hold the pieces of glass in place.

Soldering

- Your solder seam should be as tall as it is wide. You don't want it to be flat. You want it to have a crowned, rounded edge to it.
- A nice thing about copper foil soldering is that if you're not happy with the way it looks, you can just re-flux and go back over it again.

- Always keep a hot liquid puddle right under your soldering tip. Let the solder flow at its own speed along with you.
- If your solder looks lumpy, you either need more flux or more heat.
- Solder from top to bottom. I like to start at the top of my window (the part that's farthest away from me) so I don't drag my sleeves through the hot solder as I go along.

Working with the Grain of the Glass

Like fabric, art glass has a grain to it. The grain runs vertically from top to bottom on a sheet of glass. In some glass types, the striations are more visible than others. It is important to take the time to determine the grain of your glass and mark the direction of the grain by drawing arrows on your glass. The arrows will help you position the pattern pieces on the glass so they will flow with the grain.

Using the Glass Grain to Advantage:

- The grain in a window should always follow the longest direction of the window. For example, if your panel is 36" tall and 12" wide, run the grain vertically. If you are making a transom 12" tall and 36" wide, run the grain horizontally. This design principle applies to the border pieces of a design as well.
- When you are making a floral or wildlife window, it's best to imitate nature as closely as possible. For example, on a flower the grain would run from the center of the flower out.

Glass Projects You Can Do in an Afternoon

The projects in this section are stained glass projects that even a beginner can make in an afternoon, including panels, frames, boxes, and other tabletop accessories, as well as mosaics made with stained glass.

Each project includes one or more photographs, a list of supplies you'll need, and step-by-step instructions for cutting, assembling, and finishing. The Supplies list for each project usually includes a listing for "Basic Tools & Supplies"—the basic tools and supplies you will need. They are listed opposite.

Basic Tools & Supplies

You will need the following tools and supplies for each of the projects you create. These will not be listed again with each individual project. The project supply listing will consist only of the glass you will need plus additional decorating supplies.

Pattern MakingSupplies:

- Pattern fixative or rubber cement
- Pencil & eraser
- Felt-tip pen or china marker
- Pattern paper
- 18" metal ruler with cork back
- Transfer paper
- Colored pencils
- Pattern shears

Glass Cutting Tools:

- Glass cutter
- Lubricating oil
- Carborundum stone or emery cloth
  Optional: Grinder
- Combination pliers
  Optional: Breaking pliers
- Running pliers
- Grozing pliers

Assembly Supplies:

- Work board
- Squaring bars
- Push pins
- Triangle with 45 degree and 90 degree angles
- Desk brush and dust pan
- Masking tape

Soldering Supplies:

- Foil Tape
- Burnisher
- Craft knife
- Soldering iron with 1/4" tip
- Rheostat
- Soldering iron stand
- Tip cleaner
- Flux and flux brush

Safety Gear:

- Safety glasses
- Face mask

Tulip Panel

This project was the project that was used to show the basic technique for creating stained glass pieces. It is a wonderful piece to start with because of it's simplicity and the resulting beauty. It requires only three colors of glass, yet the pattern pieces will allow you to experience a variety of cuts.

Size: 7-5/8" x 12"

Supplies

Glass:
White opalescent, 1 sq. ft. (for background)
Pink opalescent, 1/2 sq. ft. (for flower)
Green opalescent, 1/2 sq. ft. (for leaves/stem)

Other Supplies:
7/32" copper foil tape
4 ft. 1/8" U-shaped came
60/40 solder
Flux
Copper wire

Tools:
Basic Tools & Supplies (See list on page 41.)
Came notcher
Needlenose pliers

Step-by-Step

See the "Crafting Your First Project" section for photos that show how to construct this project.

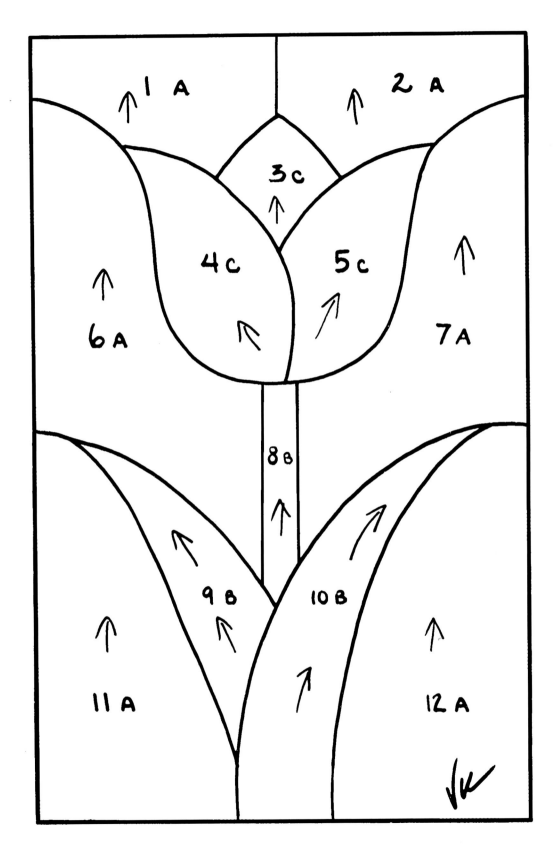

Pattern for Tulip Panel
Enlarge Pattern 148% for Actual
Size

Glass Nugget
Photo Frames

These frames are so easy you don't need a pattern! You can alter the size of a frame to fit any size photo by cutting a larger or smaller piece of clear glass and adding or subtracting the number of nuggets and jewels.

Size: Frame will accommodate a 4" x 6" photo.

Supplies

for each frame

Glass:
40-50 glass nuggets
1 or more decorative glass jewels
Clear glass, 4" x 5"

Other Supplies:
7/32" copper foil tape
60/40 solder
Flux
14" piece of 1/8" U-shaped copper came
12 gauge copper wire, 10"
Thin cardboard

Tools:
Basic Tools & Supplies (See list on page 41.)
Came notcher

Pictured on pages 44 and 45

Step-by-Step

See the photos, below.

Make the Frame:

1. Wrap the clear glass piece with copper foil.
2. Wrap each glass nugget and jewel in copper foil. *Tip:* If you have trouble getting the foil to stick to the nuggets, pass the side edge of the nugget against your grinder bit. This will give the nugget a better edge for the foil.
3. Place the clear glass piece on your work surface. Arrange the nuggets and jewels around the edge of the clear glass piece, using the photo as a guide or creating your own design.

4. Tack-solder the pieces in place.
5. Puddle-solder the nuggets to the frame.
6. To make a slot for inserting the photo, you will need to attach a piece of came to the back of the glass piece, securing it around the edge on three sides. Using the came notcher or lead nippers, measure and cut the U-shaped came to fit around the sides and bottom of the clear glass piece. Tape the came in place on the back of the frame. Solder at the four corners to secure to the frame.

Make the Frame Stand:

1. Solder one end of a 10" piece of copper wire to the side edge of the U-shaped came.
2. Using needlenose pliers, coil the other end of the copper wire into a flat spiral. Bend the spiral so it supports the frame at the angle you desire.

Finish:

1. Clean the project with soap and water.
2. Apply copper patina.
3. Cut a piece of cardboard to fit the frame as a backing for your picture. Insert photo.❖

Puddle Soldering

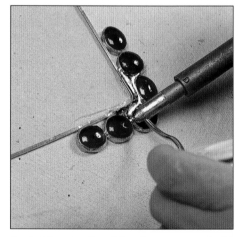

1. **Apply Foil & Assemble:** Wrap edges of clear glass, nuggets, and jewels with foil. Arrange the marbles and jewels around the edge of the clear glass piece on a heat-resistant surface, such as Homasote, stainless steel, or cement.

2. **Brush on Flux:** Apply flux to foiled areas of clear glass piece and the nuggets using a brush.

3. **Solder:** Tack-solder the pieces to hold them in place, then apply enough solder to fill in the entire space between each nugget and the clear glass piece to the top of the foil that surrounds the nugget. Don't forget to solder the outside edges. If you do a good puddle soldering job, you won't need to solder the back of the frame.

*Pattern for Crocus Panel
Pictured on page 49.*

Crocus Panel

Pattern on page 47.

On this panel, came-wrapped beveled glass pieces are soldered at the sides so the panel can be displayed on a tabletop. If you want a hanging panel, you can use wire loops and monofilament line instead. See the "Framing the Piece" section in "Crafting Your First Project" for instructions for attaching hanging loops.

Size: 7-1/2" x 9-1/4"

Supplies

Glass:
Clear textured cathedral glass, 10" x 10"
Purple cathedral glass, 6" x 8"
Green cathedral glass, 6" x 8"
2 clear glass bevels, 3" x 3" (for frame stand)

Other Supplies:
3/16" copper foil tape with black back
60/40 solder
Flux
5 ft. piece of 1/8" U-shaped zinc came
Black patina finish

Tools:
Came notcher
Basic Tools & Supplies (See list on page 41.)

Step-by-Step

Prepare, Cut & Assemble:
1. Make two copies of the pattern. Number and color-code each piece. Using pattern shears, cut out design from one copy.
2. Adhere pattern pieces to the glass. Cut out each piece.
3. Grind edges of each piece as needed to fit the pattern. Clean all glass edges.
4. On your work board, tape or pin down the second copy of the pattern. Attach squaring strips to help keep the project squared up as you assemble and solder.
5. Assemble the cut pieces of glass on top of the pattern. Use the grinder as needed to smooth edges and make adjustments. Each glass piece must fit within the pattern lines.

Apply Foil & Solder:
1. Wrap each piece of glass in 3/16" copper foil.
2. Solder pieces in place, running a nice smooth solder bead over all inside copper seams. (You do not need to solder the outside edges.) Keep the solder seams flat around the edges.
3. Turn project over and solder on the back.

Frame & Finish:
1. Using the came notcher or lead nippers, measure and cut U-shaped zinc came to frame the project and the two 3" x 3" beveled pieces.
2. Wrap the zinc came around the crocus panel and each bevel. Solder the intersections. You now have three pieces framed in zinc came.
3. Stand the panel upright, using blocks of wood, books, or coffee cans filled with sand to prop it up. Position one beveled piece at the side of the panel and solder it to the panel at the top and bottom. Repeat with the other beveled piece on the other side.
4. Clean the project with soap and water. Let dry completely.
5. Apply black patina. ❖

Fish Story

Here's one that didn't get away. Loops of copper wire and monofilament line are used to hang your catch. This is a perfect gift for the fisherman in your life. It looks great hanging in anyone's game room.

Size: 15" x 8"

Supplies

Glass:
Greenish opalescent glass, 2 sq. ft. (for body of fish)
White, brown, and gray opalescent glass, 1/4 sq. ft. of each color (for belly, mouth, and eye)
Brown ripple glass, 1 sq. ft. (for fins)

Other Supplies:
7/32" copper foil tape
60/40 solder
Flux
Black patina finish
12 gauge copper wire

Tools:

Basic Tools & Supplies (See list on page 41.)
Roundnose pliers

Instructions continued on page 52.

Continued from page 50.

Step-by-Step

Prepare, Cut & Assemble:

1. Make two copies of the pattern. Number and color-code each piece. Using pattern shears, cut out design from one copy.
2. Adhere pattern pieces to the glass. Cut out each piece.
3. Grind edges of each piece as needed to fit the pattern. Clean all glass edges.
4. On your work board, tape or pin the second copy of the pattern. Lay the cut pieces of glass on the pattern. Use the grinder to smooth edges and make adjustments. Each glass piece must fit within the pattern lines.

Apply Foil & Solder:

1. Wrap each piece of glass in 7/32" copper foil.
2. Pin pieces in place on work board, using push pins. Since this is not a square or rectangular piece, you will not be able to use squaring bars to keep the pieces in place.
3. Tack-solder pieces in place. This will help to stabilize the piece and keep pieces from slipping as you solder the piece.
4. Solder all seams, running a smooth solder bead over all inside and outside copper seams and edges.
5. Turn project over and solder the back.

Finish:

1. Using roundnose pliers, make two loops of copper wire. Solder at the vertical seams on the fish as shown on the pattern.
2. Clean the project with soap and water. Let dry completely.
3. Apply black patina. ❖

Pattern for Fish Story
Enlarge to 146% for actual size

Peacock Lampshade

Panel lampshades are unique in design—the individual panels are assembled and soldered completely before they are put together. You can vary the size and shape of the shade by adding or subtracting panels. (This shade has eight.) Lampshades may be suspended from a chain or displayed on a base. Both styles are assembled the same way.

Shades are attached to fixtures or lamp bases with a vase cap or strap bar. I recommend using base caps because they are more versatile—they can be used either way. Vase caps are available in a wide variety of sizes and designs. If you plan to use a higher wattage light bulb, be sure to select a ventilated vase cap.

This shade is made mostly of opalescent glass, which diffuses light. If you make a shade entirely of cathedral glass, your light bulb will show through the glass when the lamp or fixture is in use.

Size: 7" high, 12-3/4" diameter

Supplies

Glass:
Light green/light blue opalescent 12" x 12" (for background)

Dark green opalescent, 12" x 24" (for feathers)

Purple cathedral, 8" x 8" (for "eyes" of feathers)

Amber cathedral glass, 8" x 8" (for pieces around vase cap)

Other Supplies:
3/16" copper foil tape with black back

60/40 solder

Flux

Black patina finish

Vase cap

16 gauge copper wire (for reinforcing the shade)

Tools:
Basic Tools & Supplies (See list on page 41.)

Cardboard box or sandbags, for assembling (See below.)

Step-by-Step

Prepare, Cut & Assemble:
1. Make 16 copies of the pattern. Number and color-code each pattern piece. Using pattern shears, cut out the design from eight copies—one for each panel.
2. Adhere pattern pieces to the glass. Cut out each piece.
3. Grind edges of each piece as needed to fit the pattern. Clean all glass edges.
4. On your work board, tape or pin the other copies of the pattern. Position two squaring bars as shown in *Fig. 1*.
5. Lay the cut pieces of glass on the pattern. Use the grinder to smooth edges and make adjustments. Each glass piece must fit within the pattern lines. After you finish one panel, move on to the next one. Repeat until all eight panels are assembled.

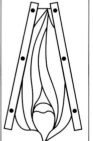

Fig. 1 - How to use squaring bars for assembling.

Apply Foil & Solder:
1. Wrap each piece of glass in 7/32" copper foil.
2. Pin pieces in place on work board, using squaring bars and push pins.
3. Tack-solder pieces in place.
4. Run a smooth solder bead over all inside and outside copper seams and edges.
5. Turn panels over and solder the backs.

Assemble the Shade:
Make sure the edges of each panel are smooth and free of any excess solder before you start this process.
1. Clean the panels with glass cleaner and a paper towel to remove the flux and allow masking tape to stick to the glass.
2. Lay out the panels on your work surface, right side down. Check closely to make sure you haven't flipped a panel the wrong way. Keep the top and the bottom edges of each panel even with those of the next panel. *See Photo 1.*
3. Check to make sure the designs match up from one panel to another. If your designs don't match up, now is the time to remake a bad panel or adjust your design.
4. Criss-cross masking tape over the back

Instructions continued on page 56.

Instructions continued from page 54.

of each panel. The more tape you use, the easier the shade will be to assemble. Make sure your tape adheres firmly to the panels. *See Photo 2.* Cut four or five extra pieces of masking tape and have them ready for the next step.

5. Holding the top edge of the two outside panels, lift the top of the shade up and off the table and into its upright position. *See Photo 3.* Secure the two meeting panels with tape. Adjust the position of the panels to assure a rounded shape and secure with more tape.

Solder the Shade:

1. Apply flux to the top of the shade and tack solder each panel to the adjacent panel.

2. Gently rotate the shade and stand it on its neck. *Caution:* **Never** lay the shade on its side—that will flatten the shade and pull the foil from the glass.

3. With the shade in this position, check the bottom of the panels and adjust the shape as needed. Return the shade to its original position. Fill each seam, from top to bottom, with solder. Don't be concerned with looks for now— you just want to make sure the shade is sturdy and will hold its shape during the beading stage.

4. Using a cardboard box or sandbags, position the shade so it can be level. (*Fig. 2*) Make sure the shade is secure and there is no pressure moving it out of shape. Apply flux to the seam and solder a smooth, level bead of solder. Allow this seam to cool. Rotate the shade to expose the next seam.
   - If the hot solder drips though the seam, turn down the temperature of your iron.
   - If your seam is pasty and lumpy

looking, turn up the temperature.
   - If you still have difficulty, move to another seam and allow the problem area to cool down.

5. When you have soldered all the outside seams, lay the shade on its side and solder the inside seams.

Reinforce the Shade:

All shades should be reinforced with copper wire for additional support and durability. Always stretch copper wire before you use it—stretching gives the wire additional strength and removes any twists or kinks.

1. Solder the wire around the neck and bottom of the shade. (*Fig. 3*) Tack-solder the wire in place, then add additional solder to cover the wire. Try to make this edge as smooth as possible.

Attach Vase Cap:

1. Position the vase cap on top of the lamp. Make sure it is level. Secure with masking tape.

2. Turn the shade over and, working from the inside, solder the cap to the neck support wire and vertical foil seams. Solder it securely, remember this area will receive the most stress over the years.

Finish:

1. Wash your lampshade with warm soapy water. (You can place the shade directly into a utility type sink for cleaning.) Drain and dry the shade.

2. *Option:* Apply black patina according to manufacturer's instructions.

3. Polish or buff the shade with glass wax or polish. ❖

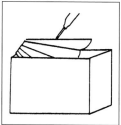

Fig. 2 - Supporting the shade for soldering with a cardboard box.

Fig. 3 - Reinforcing the shade with wire.

How to Assemble Circular Pieces

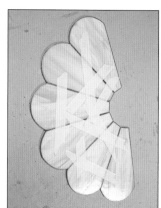

1. Lay out pieces, right sides down, on your work surface.

2. Tape pieces together on the back side, criss-crossing the tape as shown.

3. Hold upright, adjust the shape, and secure with tape before soldering.

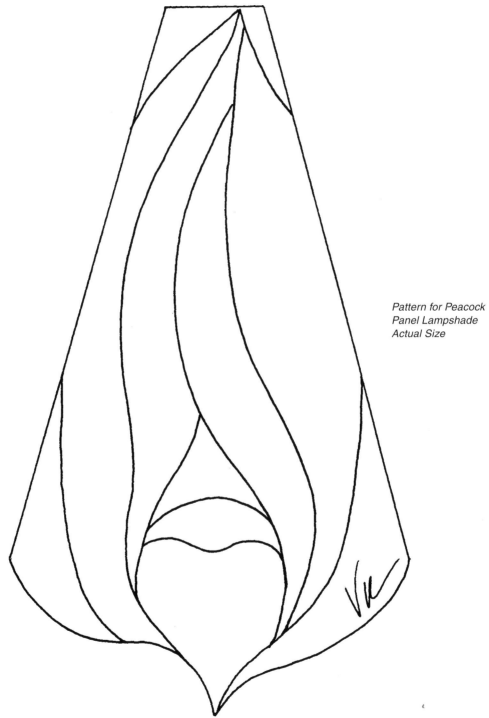

*Pattern for Peacock
Panel Lampshade
Actual Size*

Mailbox Post Decoration

This shining sun ornament fits under the supporting arm of a standard mailbox post. The contrast in the colors makes it visible even in low light. Now every day can be a sunny day at your house!

Size: 10-1/2" wide, 12" tall

Instructions begin on page 60.

Pictured on page 58,59

Supplies

Glass:
Blue cathedral glass, 10" x 10" (for background)
Yellow cathedral glass, 10" x 10" (for sun and rays)

Other Supplies:
7/32" copper foil tape
60/40 solder
Flux
4 ft. piece of 3/8" zinc came
Black patina
2 eye hooks and screws (for attaching to mailbox post)
Optional: Clear silicone caulk

Tools:
Basic Tools & Supplies (See list on page 41.)
Hacksaw with metal blade
Needlenose pliers
Optional: Electric drill

Step-by-Step

Prepare, Cut & Assemble:
1. Make two copies of the pattern. Number and color-code each piece. Using pattern shears, cut out design from one copy.
2. Adhere pattern pieces to the glass and cut out each piece.
3. Grind edges of each piece as needed each piece to fit the pattern. Clean all glass edges.
4. On your work board, tape or pin down the second copy of the pattern. Lay out the cut pieces of glass. Use your grinder to smooth edges and make adjustments. Each glass piece must fit within the pattern lines.

Apply Foil & Solder:
1. Wrap each piece of glass in 7/32" copper foil.
2. Pin pieces in place, using push pins and wooden strips to hold them securely.
3. Tack-solder pieces in place.
4. Run a smooth solder bead over all inside copper seams. You do not need to solder the outside edges. Keep the solder seams flat at the edges so the came frame will slide on easily.
5. Turn project over and solder the back.

Frame & Finish:
1. Using a hacksaw with a 32-tooth blade, cut the 3/8" U-shaped zinc came to frame the project. First cut the long edge and fit the came in place. Then cut the top and side pieces, making them long enough to extend to the edges of the came on the long edge.
2. Fit the came on the sides of the sconce. Solder at the intersections.
3. Insert the eye hooks into the ends of the zinc came on the top and bottom edges and solder in place.
4. Clean the project with soap and water. Dry completely.
5. Apply black patina according to manufacturer's instructions.

Install:
1. Position the piece under the support arm of your mailbox post and mark the location of the screw holes.
2. Pre-drill the holes, using a bit that is slightly smaller than the screws you will be using.
3. Screw the piece in place.
4. *Option:* Run a bead of clear silicone caulk between the edges of the piece and the post for additional support and a professional look. ❖

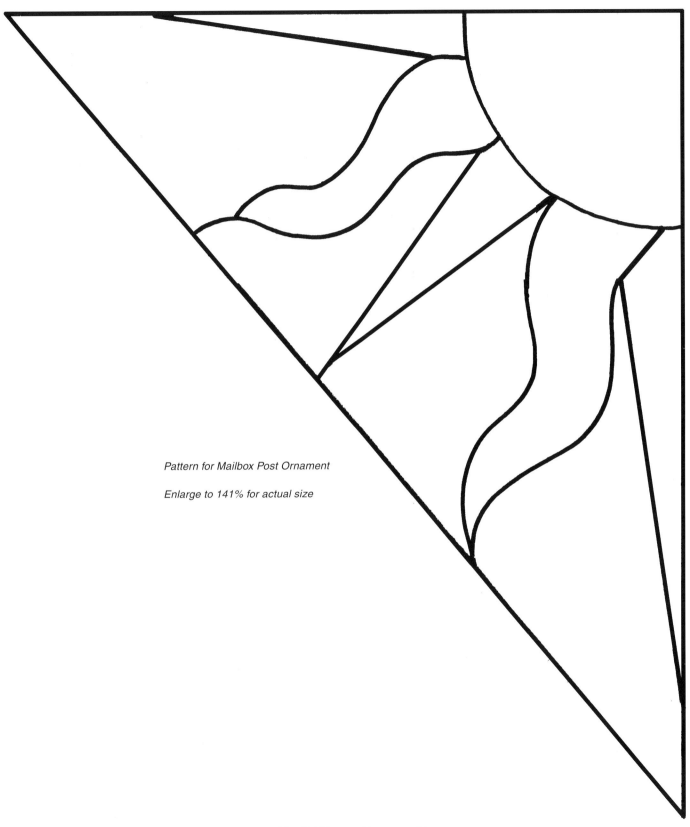

Pattern for Mailbox Post Ornament

Enlarge to 141% for actual size

Hanging Clown

Hang this circus clown's face in a window to create a dramatic focal point or obscure a less-than-inviting view. Ribbon accents add color and supply a three-dimensional look.

Size: 14" x 14"

Instructions begin on page 64.

Pictured on page 62, 63

Supplies

Glass:

White textured or rippled opalescent glass, 2 sq. ft. (for collar)

Amber opalescent, 6" x 8" (for face)

Black cathedral glass, 6" x 8" (for hat and eyes)

Red cathedral glass, 6" x 6" (for collar trim and mouth)

Other Supplies:

3/16" copper foil tape

60/40 solder

Flux

12 gauge copper wire

Black patina finish

Ribbon or monofilament line (for hanging)

Optional: Narrow red, black, and white ribbons for accents

Tools:

Basic Tools & Supplies (See list on page 41.)

Roundnose pliers

Step-by-Step

Prepare, Cut & Assemble:

1. Make two copies of your pattern. Number and color-code each piece. Using pattern shears, cut out design from one copy.
2. Adhere pattern pieces to the glass and cut out each piece.
3. Grind the edges of each piece as needed to fit the pattern. Clean all glass edges.
4. On your work board, tape or pin down the second copy of the pattern. Lay out the cut pieces of glass. Use the grinder to smooth edges and make adjustments. Each glass piece must fit within the pattern lines.

Apply Foil & Solder:

1. Wrap each piece of glass in 3/16" copper foil.
2. Pin pieces in place on work board over pattern, using push pins.
3. Tack-solder pieces in place.
4. Run a smooth solder bead over all inside copper seams. Turn the piece over and solder the back.

Finish:

1. Form loops from copper wire and solder to back of panel.
2. Clean the project with soap and water. Dry completely.
3. Apply black patina according to manufacturer's instructions.
4. *Option:* Accent the panel with ribbons tied through hangers.
5. Hang with ribbon or monofilament line. ❖

*Pattern for Hanging Clown
Enlarge 187% for actual size*

Sunflower Clock

For this clock, I drilled a hole in the center piece for the clock works with a diamond core drill bit, which is available at stained glass stores and tool centers. Instructions for drilling the glass are provided. If you don't want to drill a hole, cut the sunflower center into four pieces (shown on pattern with dotted lines), wrap with foil, and solder together before proceeding with the design.

The clock was framed in a 15" octagonal frame. You can find these frames at stained glass stores and craft shops. You could, instead, use a round or square frame and make a round or square clock, adjusting the pattern to fit the shape of the frame.

Size: 13-3/4" octagon

Supplies

Glass:
Yellow opalescent glass, various shades, 2 sq. ft.
Green opalescent glass, 1-1/2 sq. ft.
Brown opalescent glass, 8" x 8"

Other Supplies:
3/16" copper foil tape with black back
60/40 solder
Flux
Copper or black patina finish
Battery-operated clockworks with hands
Wooden frame
Clear silicone caulk
Plastic dish or container, 9" diameter or larger
Cellulose sponge

Tools:

Basic Tools & Supplies (See list on page 41.)
1/4" diamond core drill bit (or the size to fit your clockworks)
Electric drill or Dremel Tool

Step-by-Step

Prepare & Cut:
1. Make two copies of your pattern. Number and color-code each piece. Using pattern shears, cut out design from one copy.
2. Adhere pattern pieces to the glass. Cut out each piece.
3. Grind the edges of each piece as needed to fit the pattern. Clean all glass edges.

Drill the Hole:
It is a good idea to practice this technique before attempting to drill your actual piece.
1. To keep the glass cooled with water while drilling, use a 9" diameter or larger plastic container or dish as a drilling station. Place a wet sponge on the bottom of the container to cushion the glass and absorb the shock of the drill passing through the glass.
2. Mark the center of the glass circle with a fine tip marker or china marker. Place glass circle into the dish on top of the wet sponge. Add enough water to cover the sponge and the glass, but not deeper than 1/8" above the glass surface.
3. Using an electric drill or Dremel tool fitted with a diamond core drill bit large enough to accommodate the stem on your clockworks, drill the hole in the glass.

4. Remove the glass and wipe dry.

Assemble:
1. On your work board, tape or pin down the second copy of the pattern. Lay out the cut pieces of glass.
2. Use the grinder to smooth the edges and make adjustments. Each glass piece must fit within the pattern lines.

Apply Foil & Solder:
1. Wrap each piece of glass in 3/16" copper foil.
2. Pin pieces in place over the pattern, using push pins.
3. Tack-solder pieces in place.
4. Run a smooth solder bead over all inside copper seams. Be sure to solder the outside edges of the foiled pieces to add strength to the project.
5. Turn the project over and solder the back.

Finish:
1. Clean the project with soap and water. Dry completely.
2. Apply patina according to manufacturer's instructions.
3. Following the manufacturer's instructions, install the clockworks.
4. Place the clock in the wooden frame. Secure it in place with a bead of clear silicone caulk. ❖

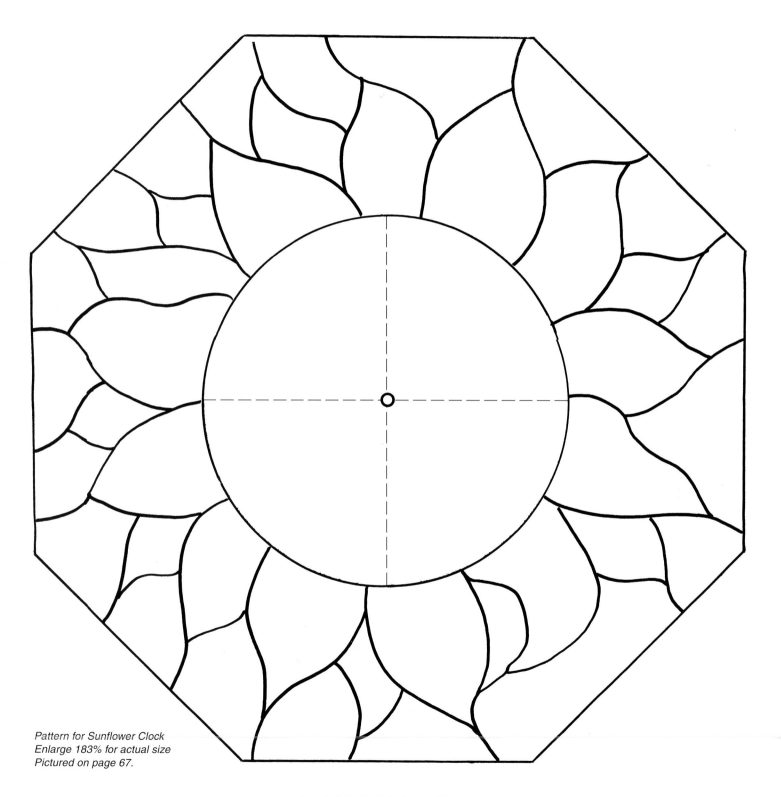

*Pattern for Sunflower Clock
Enlarge 183% for actual size
Pictured on page 67.*

Pattern for Front of Bluebird Birdhouse
Actual Size
Pictured on page 71.

Patterns continue on pages 72 and 73.

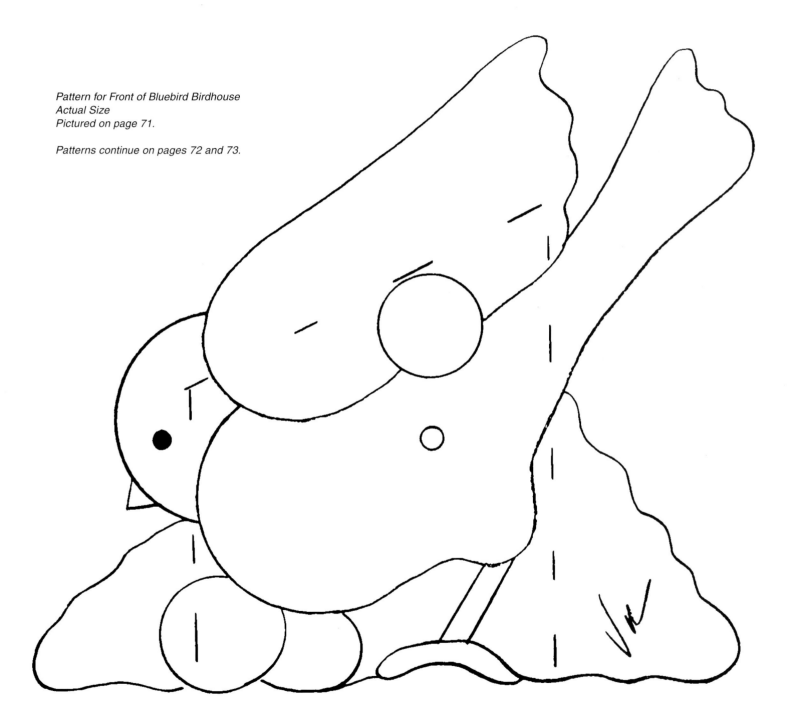

Bluebird Birdhouse

Pattern on page 69

This birdhouse was designed to be used indoors or outdoors for decorative purposes only. If you would like to hang your birdhouse, attach a wire loop on the long side of the back about 2" down from the top. Check the balance and adjust the placement as needed to get it to hang straight.

Size: 5-1/4" deep x 7" tall x 7-1/2" wide

Supplies

Glass:
White, 5" x 20" (for birdhouse)
Blue, 8" x 8" (for the bird)
Light blue, 3" x 3" (for the eggs)
Green, 4" x 5" (for the grass)

Other Supplies:
7/32" copper foil tape
8 ft. 1/8" U-shaped zinc came
60/40 solder
Flux

Tools:

Basic Tools & Supplies (See list on page 41.)
Came notcher

Step-by-Step

Prepare & Cut:
1. Make two copies of your pattern. Number and color-code each piece. Using pattern shears, cut out design from one copy.
2. Adhere pattern pieces to the glass. Cut out each piece.
3. Grind the edges of each piece as needed to fit the pattern. Clean all glass edges.

Assemble the Bluebird:
1. On your work board, tape or pin down the second copy of the bluebird pattern. Lay out the cut pieces of glass.
2. Use the grinder to smooth the edges and make adjustments. Each glass piece must fit within the pattern lines.

Apply Foil to Bluebird & Solder:
1. Wrap each piece of glass for the bird in 7/32" copper foil.
2. Pin pieces in place on the pattern, using push pins.
3. Tack-solder pieces in place.
4. Run a smooth solder bead over all inside and outside copper seams and edges.
5. Use the tip of your soldering iron to build up a small bead of solder on the outside edge of the assembled bluebird.
6. Turn project over. Solder the back.

Frame & Solder the Birdhouse:
1. Using the came notcher or lead nippers, measure and cut the 1/8" U-shaped zinc came to frame each piece of the birdhouse.
2. Wrap the came around each piece and tack-solder the ends where they meet.
3. To assemble the birdhouse, place the floor on your work board. Working one at a time, place the two side pieces around it and tack-solder them in place.
4. Position the back of the birdhouse on the floor and between the two side sections and tack-solder in place. The pieces should meet along the top.
5. Position the roof of the birdhouse as shown in Fig. 1. Keep it flush with the top edge of side A and allow the roof to overhang side B by about 3/16". Tack-solder in place.

Finish:
1. Clean the project completely with soap and water.
2. Attach the front (the bluebird) to the birdhouse by soldering where the foil seams intersect with the zinc came.
3. Clean up any flux residue. ❖

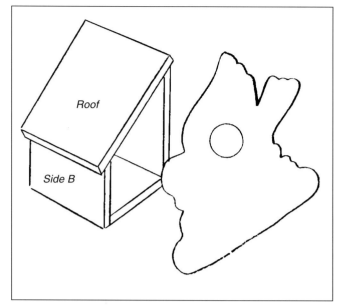

Fig. 1- Assembling the birdhouse

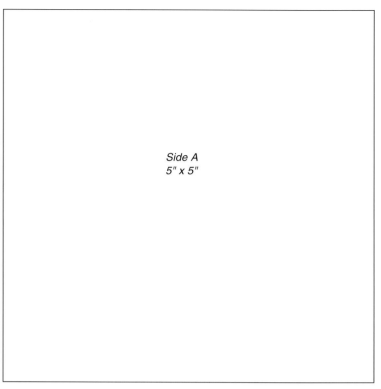

Side A
5" x 5"

Roof
5" x 5"

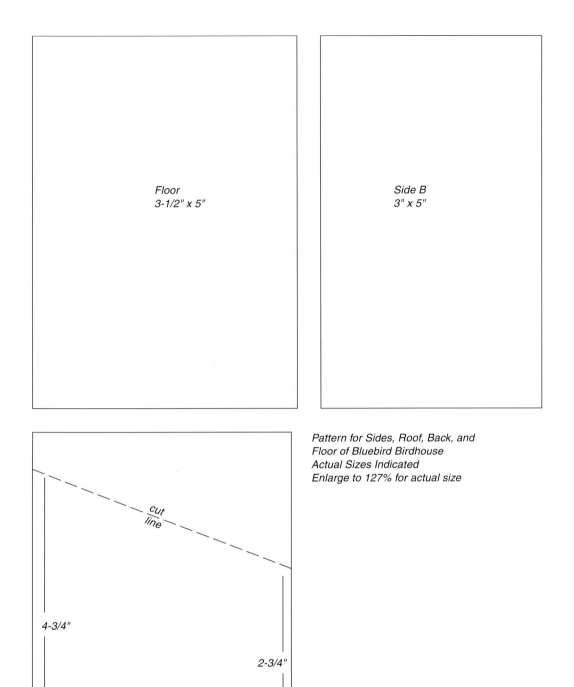

Floor
3-1/2" x 5"

Side B
3" x 5"

Pattern for Sides, Roof, Back, and
Floor of Bluebird Birdhouse
Actual Sizes Indicated
Enlarge to 127% for actual size

cut
line

4-3/4"

2-3/4"

Back
3-1/2" x 5"

Dancing Women Candleholders

These candlesticks have a frame of zinc rebar. The rebar is fairly easy to bend with your hands, but you may need to use pliers to achieve some of the curves. A ring at the bottom forms the base of each candlestick; a ring at the top holds a glass candle cup for a votive candle.

I used a kind of glass called Spectrum Baroque because of its bold stripes. The abstract design recalls women walking with their arms aloft, carrying the candle cups.

Size: 14" tall

Supplies

Glass:
Striped Spectrum Baroque, 10" x 10"
2 large glass nuggets

Other Supplies:
7/32" copper foil tape with black back
4 strips of zinc rebar, each 16"
4 brass rings, 2-1/2" diameter
12 gauge copper wire, 2"
60/40 solder
Flux
Black patina finish
2 glass votive candle cups (They should fit securely in the brass rings.)
Red marker
Jewelry glue

Tools:

Basic Tools & Supplies (See list on page 41.)
Wooden work board
Nails
Hammer
Needlenose pliers

Step-by-Step

Shape Rebar Strips:
1. Tape your pattern to a wooden work board. Bend the zinc rebar to match the pattern as closely as you can. Use nails to hold the zinc in place as you bend it.
2. Outline the shape of the rebar on the pattern with a red marker. Adjust the pattern if necessary to match the shape of the rebar.

Prepare, Cut & Assemble:
1. Make two copies of your adjusted pattern. Using scissors, cut out design from one copy.
2. Adhere pattern pieces to the glass, selecting sections of the glass that resemble folds in fabric to create the figures' "clothes." Cut out each piece.
3. Grind the edges of each piece to fit the pattern as needed. Clean all glass edges.
4. On your work board, tape or pin down the pattern. Lay out the cut pieces of glass next to the shaped rebar. Be sure the glass edges touch the rebar all the way down both sides. Use the grinder to adjust as needed.

Apply Foil & Solder:
1. Wrap each piece of glass in 7/32" copper foil.
2. Pin pieces in place, using push pins or nails.
3. Tack-solder pieces in place.
4. Run a smooth solder bead over all the seams.
5. Turn project over and solder the back.

Finish:
1. Cut 1/2" pieces of copper wire for the necks and solder in place.
2. Tin the four brass rings with solder. To tin, brush the metal with flux and coat with a thin layer of solder. (This is so the rings will accept the black patina and match your project.)
3. To attach the base ring on each candlestick, place the tinned brass ring on your work board and position the candlestick inside the ring. Tack-solder the back of the holder to the edge of the ring as shown on the pattern. Make sure the candlestick and ring are level so the candlestick will stand up.
4. To attach the top ring, stand your candlestick upright and hold the tinned brass ring with needlenose pliers. Make sure the ring is level and touching both strips of rebar. Tack-solder in place. **Caution:** Brass is a very fast conductor of heat. Do not hold the ring with your fingers—you will burn your hand!
5. Check to be sure the ring and votive holder fit securely and are level. Adjust if needed.
6. Glue nuggets to wire "necks" with jewelry glue.
7. Clean the project with soap and water. Dry completely.
8. Apply black patina. ❖

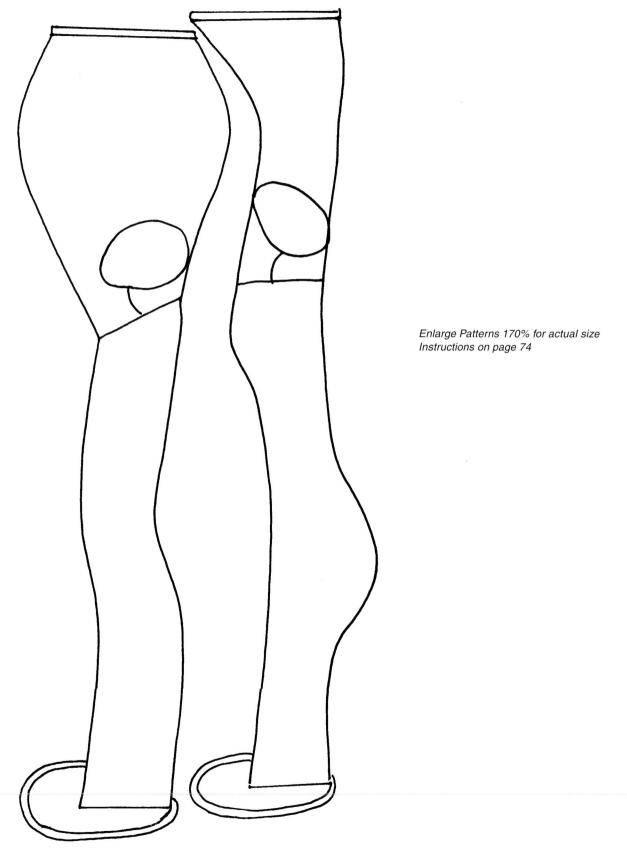

Enlarge Patterns 170% for actual size
Instructions on page 74

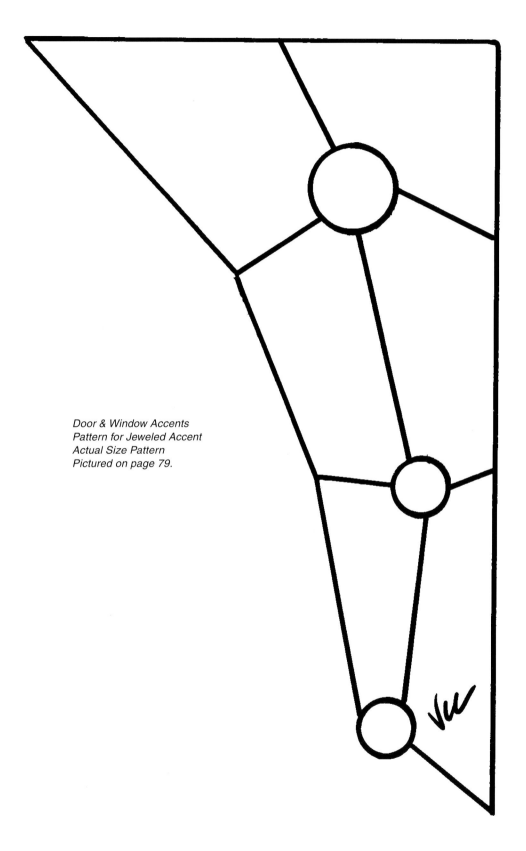

Door & Window Accents
Pattern for Jeweled Accent
Actual Size Pattern
Pictured on page 79.

Door & Window Accents

Use these accents to add color and design to French doors and windows. They can be added to outside or inside corners.

Included here are a simple rose design, a freeform design with glass nuggets and jewels, and a design made from pre-cut beveled glass pieces that's extra easy—neither cutting nor a pattern is required!

The most important tip I can give you for making these fun accent pieces is to make sure the corner is a perfect 90-degree angle so the piece will fit snugly in a door or windowpane.

Size: 5" x 8"

Supplies

Glass:
For the Rose Accent:
Pale pink opalescent, 5" x 8" (for the background)
Pink opalescent, 5" x 6" (for the rose)
Green, 5" x 6" (for the leaves)

For the Jeweled Accent:
Yellow cathedral glass, 8" x 8"
3 jewels or nuggets

For the Beveled Accent:
Squares - one 2", one 1"
Rectangles - one 1" x 2", one 1" x 3", one 1" x 4", one 1" x 5"

Other Supplies:
7/32" copper foil tape
60/40 solder
Flux
13" of 1/8" zinc, brass, or copper U-shaped came for each piece
Optional: Patina finish
Optional: Clear silicone adhesive, duct tape, wire loops, small screws (See "Install," below.)

Tools:
Basic Tools & Supplies (See list on page 41.)
Came notcher
Optional: Drill and drill bit (See "Install," below.)

Step-by-Step

Prepare & Cut:
The instructions in this section apply only to the Rose Accent and the Jeweled Accent. The Beveled Accent does not require a pattern or cutting.

1. Make two copies of your pattern. Number and color-code each piece. Using pattern shears, cut out design from one copy.
2. Adhere pattern pieces to the glass and cut out each piece.
3. Grind each piece to fit the pattern. Clean all glass edges.
4. On your work board tape or pin down the second copy of the pattern. Lay out the cut pieces of glass. Use your grinder to smooth out the edges and make any necessary adjustments. Each glass piece must fit within the pattern lines.

Apply Foil & Solder:
1. Wrap each piece of glass in 7/32" copper foil.
2. Pin pieces in place, using push pins and wooden strips to keep your corner a perfect 90-degree angle.
3. Tack-solder pieces in place.
4. Run a smooth solder bead over all inside copper seams. You do not need to solder the outside edges of the two sides that form the 90 degree angle. Keep the solder seams flat on the straight edges of the project so the came frame will slide on easily.
5. Turn project over and solder the back.

Frame & Finish:
1. Using the came notcher or lead nippers, measure and cut the 1/8" U-shaped came to frame the sides that form the 90 degree angle.
2. Slip the came onto these sides and solder the corner and each end.
3. Clean the project with soap and water. Dry completely.
4. *Option:* Apply patina.

Install:
Option #1:
1. Tape the piece in place using duct tape.
2. Run a smooth bead of clear silicone where the glass and wood moldings meet. Let dry overnight. Remove the tape.

Option #2:
1. Solder small wire loops to the top and bottom edge of the came frame.
2. Pre-drill the holes in the molding (to avoid splitting the wood) and use small screws to attach the accent piece to the moldings. ❖

Pictured at right: accent shown on a framed mirror.

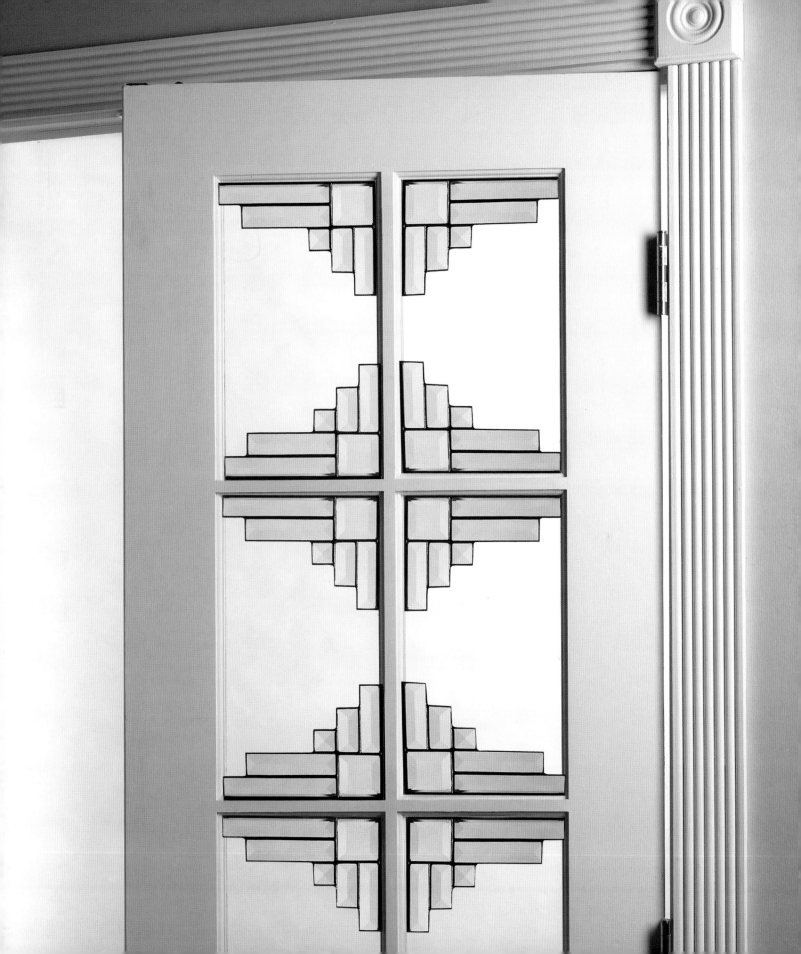

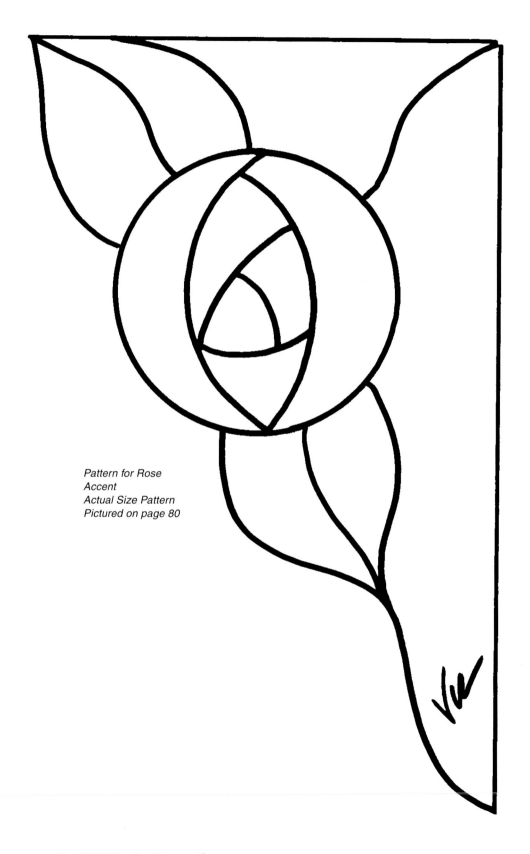

*Pattern for Rose
Accent
Actual Size Pattern
Pictured on page 80*

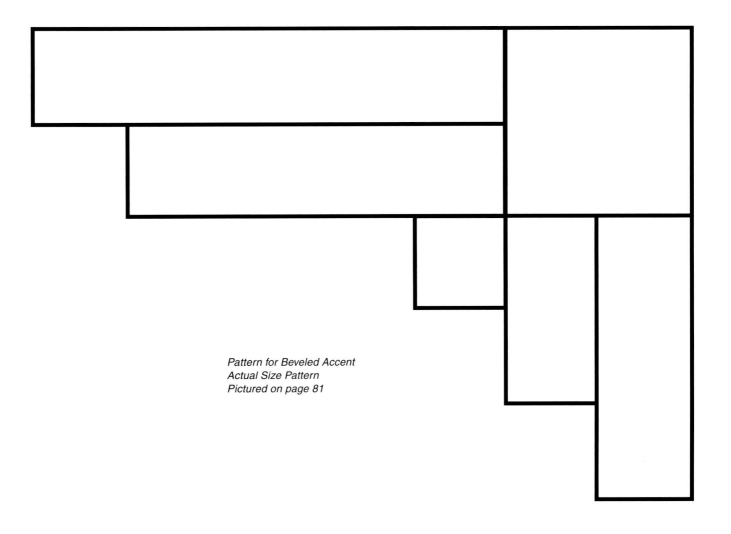

Pattern for Beveled Accent
Actual Size Pattern
Pictured on page 81

Orange Blossom Corner Accent

This project can be made as a single piece or a pair. The supplies listed will make one piece. To make a pair, flip the pattern and use a light box to copy the design to make a pair of mirror images. If you like, add a little variety to the second design by changing the design elements just a little. It's easier than you think to design your own piece. Since this piece is a little more advanced, it may take several afternoons to complete.

Size: 21" x 18"

Instructions begin on page 86.

Continued from page 84.

Supplies

Glass:

Green opalescent and cathedral, 2 sq. ft. (Using various shades of green glass will make this project really beautiful.)

Bright orange cathedral, 6" x 6"

Medium orange opalescent, 6" x 6"

White opalescent, 6" x 6"

2 yellow nuggets

Clear cathedral, 6" x 6"

Other Supplies:

3/16" copper foil tape

60/40 solder

Flux

3-1/2 ft. piece of 1/2" U-shaped zinc came

2 eye hooks, 3/8"

2 wood screws

Black patina finish

Copper patina finish

Optional: Clear silicone adhesive

Tools:

Basic Tools & Supplies (See list on page 41.)

Hacksaw with metal blade to cut zinc came

Needlenose pliers

Step-by-Step

Prepare & Cut:

1. Make two copies of your pattern. Number and color-code each piece. Using pattern shears, cut out design from one copy.
2. Adhere pattern pieces to the glass. Cut out each piece.
3. Grind the edges of each piece as needed to fit the pattern. Clean all glass edges.
4. On your work board tape or pin down the second copy of the pattern. Lay out the cut pieces of glass. Use your grinder to smooth edges and make adjustments. Each glass piece must fit within the pattern lines.

Apply Foil & Solder:

1. Wrap each piece of glass in 3/16" copper foil.
2. Place pieces over pattern and pin in place, using push pins and wooden strips.
3. Tack-solder pieces in place.
4. Run a smooth solder bead over all inside copper seams. You do not need to solder the straight edges. Keep the solder seams flat around the straight edges so the came frame will slide on easily.
5. Turn project over. Solder the back.

Frame & Finish:

1. Using a hacksaw, cut two pieces of zinc came, one 21" and one 18" long. *Tip:* It will look best if you miter the corner where the pieces join. If you decide not to miter the intersection, add 1/2" to one of the pieces.

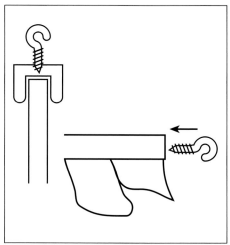

Fig. 1 - Attaching the eye hooks.

2. Solder the zinc came to the panel at each spot where a foil seam meets the came. Turn over the panel and solder the back where the seams touch the came.
3. Insert an eye hook in the back of the channel. See Fig. 1. Hold with needlenose pliers and solder in place. Add a second hook to the top edge.
4. Clean the project with soap and water. Dry completely.
5. Apply black patina to the foil seams and copper patina to the zinc came, following manufacturer's instructions. (Copper patina turns zinc came black.)

Install:

Insert a wood screw through the eye hook and screw to wood molding. Add a small dab of clear silicone adhesive at the top corner to add stability. ❖

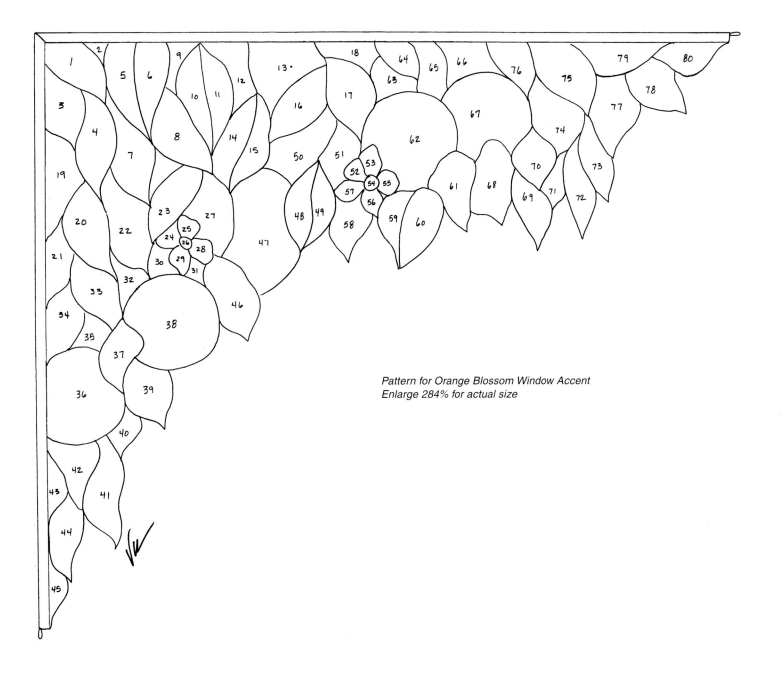

Pattern for Orange Blossom Window Accent
Enlarge 284% for actual size

Garden Cloches

Cloches—also called "garden bells"—were traditionally used outdoors to protect tender plants from the weather. These hexagonal cloches, shown in two sizes, are made from clear glass. Each piece of glass is framed with U-shaped brass came and the pieces are soldered together to form the shape. Glass beads are used to decorate the tops and give the effect of a finial. They are so pretty you might want to use them indoors as decorative accents.

Large Size: 13" x 7-1/2"
Small Size: 7" x 5-1/2"

Supplies

Glass:
For small cloche:
Clear or textured, 9" x 30"
Optional: Glass beads

For large cloche:
Clear or textured, 14" x 38"
Optional: Glass beads

Other Supplies:
Small cloche - 18 ft. of 1/8" U-shaped brass came
Large cloche - 24 ft. of 1/8" U-shaped brass came
50/50 or 60/40 solder
Flux
Gold paint pen for coloring solder joints
Masking tape
Optional: 18 gauge brass wire (for beads)

Tools:

Basic Tools & Supplies (See list on page 41.)
Came notcher

Continued on page 90.

Continued from page 88.

Step-by-Step for Any Size Garden Cloche

Cut:

1. Adhere roof pattern to glass and cut out pieces.
2. Cut out sides. *For the small cloche,* cut six pieces, each 3" x 5". *For the large cloche,* cut six 4" x 8" pieces.

Wrap with Came & Solder:

1. Using the came notcher or lead nippers, measure and cut 1/8" brass U-shaped came to wrap each piece of glass. Solder the corner where the ends meet to secure the came. You now have 12 pieces of glass—6 side pieces and 6 roof pieces—framed in brass came.
2. Lay out the sides, placing the front side of the glass face down on your work board. Make sure the top and bottom edges are in a straight line. Tape the panels together with masking tape in a straight line so the pieces are side by side.
3. Pick up the taped-together side pieces as if they were one unit and shape into a hexagon, using the pattern as a guide. *See Fig. 1.*
4. Secure by tack-soldering the top edges where they touch. Carefully rotate the cloche, turning up so the bottom edge is on top. (At this point, it will still be a little flexible.) Adjust the sides into an even hexagon shape, again using the pattern as a guide. Secure at the corners with solder.
5. Lay out the roof pieces, placing the front side of the glass face down on your work board. Line up the edges of the roof pieces so they touch end to end. Secure with tape in a straight line — so the pieces are side by side.
6. Pick up the roof as you did the sides and shape into the same hexagon shape. Tack-solder the corners.
7. Place the roof on top of the side pieces, making sure there is a good fit. Secure with solder. *See Fig. 2.*
8. Turn the cloche over. Solder the seams inside the roof and sides to provide more stability.

Finish:

1. *Optional:* To decorate the top of the cloche, string beads on wire and insert the ends of the wire through a seam in the roof. Solder from the inside to secure.
2. Clean the project with soap and water. Dry completely.
3. Paint soldered joints with a gold paint pen so the silvery joints blend with the brass came. ❖

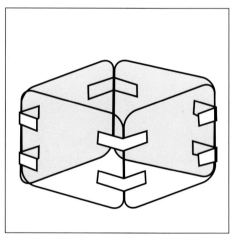

Figure 1

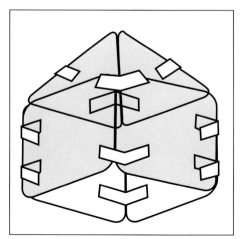

Figure 2

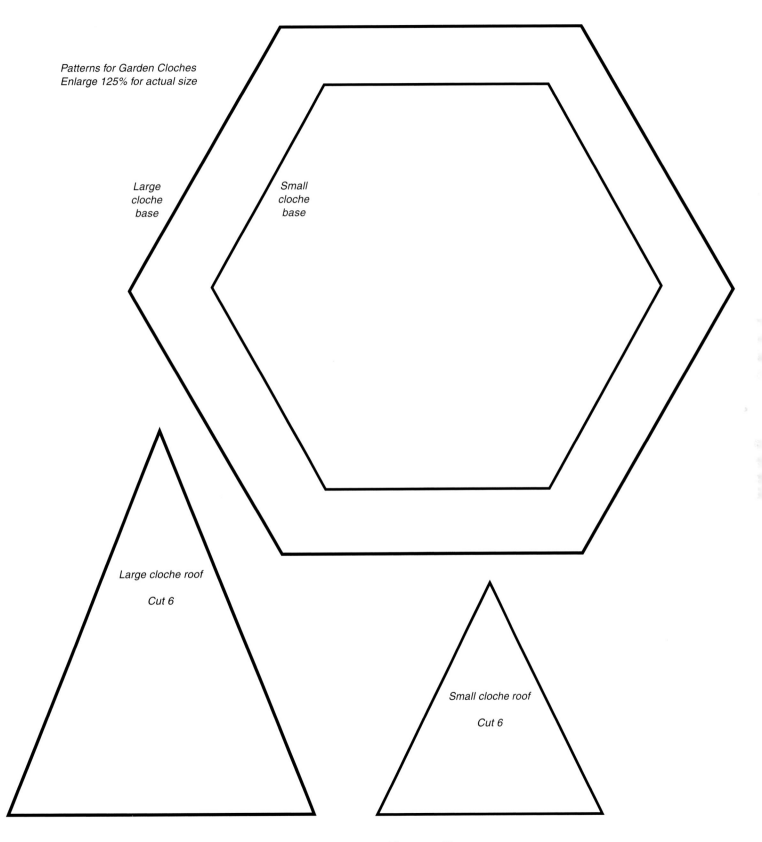

*Patterns for Garden Cloches
Enlarge 125% for actual size*

*Large
cloche
base*

*Small
cloche
base*

Large cloche roof

Cut 6

Small cloche roof

Cut 6

Beveled Candleholder Cubes

Candle cubes make wonderful gifts. This project does not require a great deal of cutting or a pattern. You can buy beveled glass pieces in a wide assortment of sizes—you will just need to cut one piece of mirror for the bottom.

You can vary the size of your cubes by using different sizes of beveled glass pieces. You could also use any type or color of art glass to make candle cubes.

Size: 4" x 4"

Supplies

Glass:
4 beveled glass pieces, 4" x 4"
Mirror, 1/8" thick, 4" x 4" (for bottom)

Other Supplies:
7/32" copper foil tape with black back
60/40 solder
Flux
Black patina finish

Tools:

Basic Tools & Supplies (See list on page 41.)

Step-by-Step

Apply Foil & Solder:
1. Wrap each of the four beveled pieces in 7/32" copper foil.
2. Assemble cube sides and tack-solder in place.
3. Check to be sure the mirror piece fits inside the cube easily. Remove the mirror. Wrap with 7/32" copper foil.
4. Place the mirror back in the bottom of the cube. Tack-solder in place.
5. Run a smooth solder bead over all inside and outside copper foil seams.

Finish:
1. Clean the project with soap and water. Dry completely.
2. Apply black patina. ❖

Star & Stripes Welcome Sign

Pattern on page 100

Red, white, and blue are combined in this circular sign. It can be hung with monofilament line or from a rebar and wire "Welcome" hanger. See page 98 for instructions for making the hanger.

Size: 10" circle

Supplies

Glass:
White opalescent, 12" x 12"
Red cathedral, 12" x 12"
Blue cathedral, 12" x 12"

Other Supplies:
3/16" copper foil tape
60/40 solder
Flux
6 ft. piece of 1/8" U-shaped zinc came
12 gauge copper wire for hanging loops

Tools:
Basic Tools & Supplies (See list on page 41.)

Step-by-Step

Prepare & Cut:
1. Make two copies of your pattern. Number and color-code each piece. Using pattern shears, cut out design from one copy.
2. Adhere pattern pieces to the glass. Cut out each piece.
3. Grind each piece as needed to fit the pattern. Clean all glass edges.
4. On your work board, tape or pin down the second copy of the pattern. Lay out the cut pieces of glass. Use the grinder to smooth out edges and make adjustments. Each glass piece must fit within the pattern lines.

Apply Foil & Solder:
1. Wrap each piece of glass in 3/16" copper foil.
2. Pin pieces in place on the pattern, using push pins.
3. Tack-solder pieces in place.
4. Run a smooth solder bead over all inside copper seams. You do not need to solder the outside edges. Keep the seams flat around the edges of the project so the came frame will slide on easily.
5. Turn over the project. Solder the back.

Frame & Finish:
1. Using the came notcher or lead nippers, measure and cut zinc came to frame the circle.
2. Wrap the came around the project. Solder where the foil seams meet the frame.
3. Attach copper wire loops to the top of the framed panel to line up with the sign holder.
4. Clean the project with soap and water. Dry completely.
5. Apply black patina according to manufacturer's instructions.
6. Attach sign to hanger with wire. ❖

Halloween Welcome Sign

Patern on page 101

Welcome trick-or-treaters to your door on Halloween with this colorful jack o'lantern. It can be hung with monofilament line or from a rebar and wire "Welcome" hanger. See page 98 for instructions for making the hanger.

Size: 10" Circle

Supplies

Glass:
Black iridized, 10" x 8" (for hat)
Dark purple or blue cathedral, 6" x 8" (for sky)
Green opalescent, 4" x 3" (for hat band)
Orange opalescent, 10" x 10" (for pumpkin)
Yellow cathedral, 6" x 8" (for eyes, nose, and mouth)

Other Supplies:
3/16" copper foil tape with black back
60/40 solder
Flux
6 ft. 1/8" U-shaped zinc came
Black patina finish
Copper wire for loops and fastening

Tools:

Basic Tools & Supplies (See list on page 41.)

Continued on page 98.

Continued from page 96.

Step-by-Step

Prepare & Cut:

1 Make two copies of your pattern. Number and color-code each piece. Using pattern shears, cut out design from one copy.

2. Adhere pattern pieces to the glass. Cut out each piece.

3. Grind each piece as needed to fit the pattern. Clean all glass edges.

4 On your work board, tape or pin down the second copy of the pattern. Lay out the cut pieces of glass. Use the grinder to smooth out edges and make adjustments. Each glass piece must fit within the pattern lines.

Apply Foil & Solder:

1. Wrap each piece of glass in 3/16" copper foil.

2. Pin pieces in place on the pattern, using push pins.

3. Tack-solder pieces in place.

4. Run a smooth solder bead over all inside copper seams. You do not need to solder the outside edges. Keep the seams flat around the edges of the project so the came frame will slide on easily.

5. Turn over the project. Solder the back.

Frame & Finish:

1. Using the came notcher or lead nippers, measure and cut zinc came to frame the circle.

2. Wrap the came around the project. Solder the where the foil seams meet the frame.

3. Attach copper wire loops to the top of the framed panel to line up with the sign holder.

4. Clean the project with soap and water. Dry completely.

5. Apply black patina according to manufacturer's instructions.

6. Attach sign to hanger with wire. ❖

Making Welcome Sign Holder

Supplies

9 gauge strand wire
12" zinc rebar (Copper or brass pieces or piping will also work.)
Copper wire for hanging loops
Black spray paint

Step-by-Step

1. Copy the pattern and pin to your work board.

2. Shape 9 gauge strand wire to fit the letters of the pattern and pin in place with push pins.

3. Bend the rebar into a gentle arch. Pin under the message.

4. Solder the two pieces together where the letters touch the arch.

5. Use copper wire to make round hanging loops for the bar. Solder them in place.

6. Paint with black spray paint. Set aside to dry. ❖

Pattern for Welcome Sign Holder
Enlarge 208% for actual size

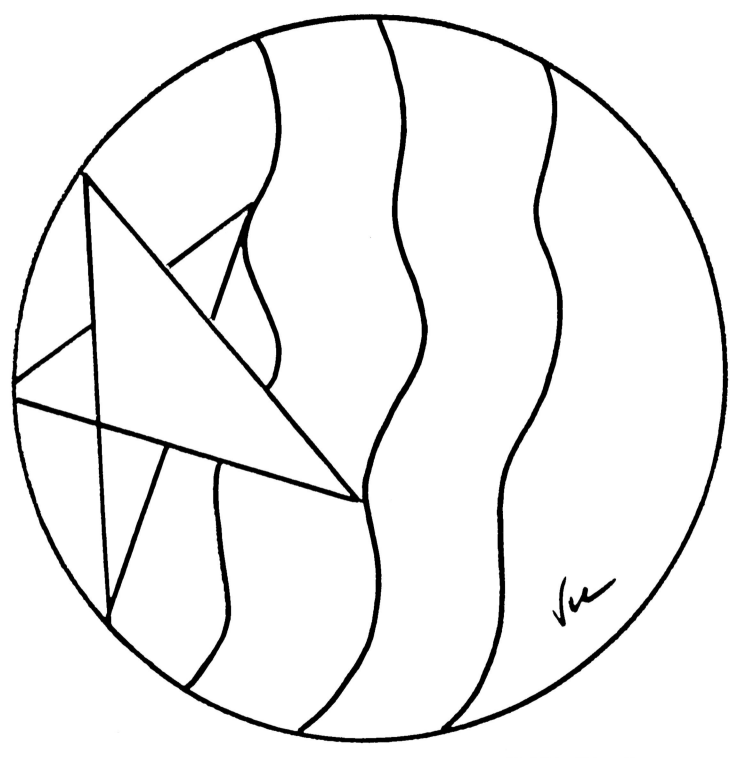

Star & Stripes Welcome Sign
Pattern - Enlarge 133% for actual size

Halloween Welcome Sign
Pattern - Enlarge 133% for actual size

General Instructions for Making Boxes

Once you learn this simple box-making technique, you can create all types and sizes of boxes. You will not need a pattern unless you want to make a box with a decorative multi-piece top.

This cutting layout (*Figure 1*) allows the grain of the glass to flow uninterrupted up the front of your box, across the top, and down the back. If the layout seems strange, just wait—as you assemble the box it will all come together and you will be delighted with the results.

Legend

SBT	Side B Top
SBB	Side B Bottom
SAT	Side A Top
SAB	Side A Bottom
BB	Back Bottom
BT	Back Top
TB	Top Back
TA	Top Front
FT	Front Top
FB	Front Bottom

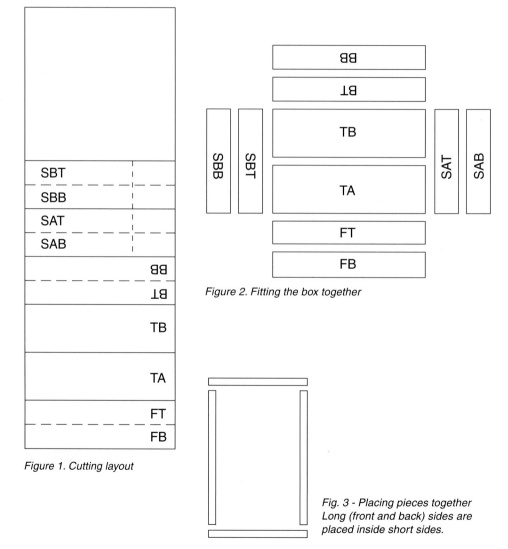

Figure 1. Cutting layout

Figure 2. Fitting the box together

Fig. 3 - Placing pieces together Long (front and back) sides are placed inside short sides.

Cutting & Assembling a Box

1. Use a strip cutter to cut the pieces of the box. If you have not worked with a strip cutter before, practice on scrap clear glass before you attempt to cut your art glass.

2. Wrap each piece with copper foil. Assemble and solder the top. Assemble the side pieces and solder at the corners to stabilize.

3. Box pieces are ready for final assembly.

Seashell Box

This box has a divided lid to allow for the seam where the seashells will be attached. The instructions are written for using a strip cutter to cut the glass. If you are not using a strip cutter, use a ruler and your hand cutter.

Size: 4" x 6"

Supplies

Glass:
Blue-green opalescent, 14" x 7"
Mirror, 1/8" thick, 4" x 6"

Other Supplies:
7/32" copper foil tape
7/32" "New Wave" foil tape
60/40 solder
Flux
1 pair box hinges
6" silver box chain
3-4 seashells

Tools:

Basic Tools & Supplies (See list on page 41.)
Glass strip cutter
Needlenose pliers

Continued on page 106.

Continued from page 104.

Step-by-Step

Cut & Assemble:

See "General Instructions for Making Boxes" before you start to cut.

1. Square up your piece of glass so all four corners are 90-degree angles. Make sure the edges are smooth and straight.
2. Mark the grain of the glass with a felt-tip marker.
3. Set your strip cutter for 2" strips. Cut one 2" x 6" strip of glass for the front of the box. Cut one 4" x 6" strip for the top. Reset your strip cutter and cut three 2" x 6" strips for the back and sides.
4. To make the shorter sides of the box, cut the side pieces (pieces labeled SA and SB in the General Instructions) to 4-1/4" long. You can use the strip cutter or cut them by hand.
5. Now you are ready to separate the four box side bottoms (pieces labeled FB, BB, SAB, and SBB in the General Instructions) from the box side tops (pieces labeled FT, BT, SAT, and SBT). Set your strip cutter for 1-3/4". Follow the layout and double check the grain markings on the glass before you cut.
6. To cut the top in two pieces, draw a gently curved line across the top of the box. Using your hand cutter, cut along this line.

7. Lay out the cut pieces of glass as shown in the General Instructions. Use a grinder to smooth the edges and make adjustments. The edges of each glass piece must be smooth and straight.

Apply Foil & Solder:

1. Wrap all the side bottom pieces and side top pieces in 7/32" copper foil.
2. Following the General Instructions, assemble the side top pieces and side bottom pieces of the box and tack-solder.
3. To assemble the top, make sure the glass edges are smooth and use 7/32" foil on the outside edges and "New Wave" foil on the inside curved seam. Make sure the top fits easily inside the top sides.
4. Run a smooth solder bead over all inside copper seams. You do not need to solder the outside edges. Turn the lid over and solder the back.
5. To assemble the bottom of the box, wrap the mirror piece in foil and place flat on the work surface, mirror side up. Place the bottom side section around the mirror. The mirror should fit easily into the box. Tack-solder the corners of the mirror to the corners of the box. Turn the box over and run a flat, smooth solder seam around the bottom edges, then solder the seams inside the box bottom.

Add Hinges:

1. Fit the top and bottom of the box together. Make sure you are happy with the fit. Secure with two rubber bands to help hold them together while you solder the hinges.
2. Position the hinges on the back of the box. Hold the hinges in place with needlenose pliers. Using a cotton swab or small paintbrush, paint flux on the edge of the hinge. *Tip:* Don't use too much flux or the solder will run into your hinge and ruin it. Remember solder can't travel where there is no flux.

Finish:

1. Solder the front and back outside seams of the box.
2. Solder a length of box chain inside the box to keep the lid from falling backward when opened.
3. Apply 7/32" copper foil to the edges of the seashells. Position the shells over the seam on the top of the box. Tack-solder the shells securely to the curved seam.
4. Clean the project with soap and water. ❖

Confetti Glass Box & Frame

Pictured on page 109

A coordinated box and frame make a wonderful duo for the top of a chest or dresser. The instructions are written for using a strip cutter to cut the glass. If you are not using a strip cutter, use a ruler and your hand cutter.

Confetti Glass Box

Sizes: Frame will accommodate a 4" x 6" photo; box is 4" x 6".

Supplies

Glass:
Confetti glass, 14" x 7"
1 triangular piece of beveled glass, 3"
Mirror, 1/8" thick, 4" x 6"

Other Supplies:
7/32" copper foil tape with silver backing
60/40 solder
Flux
1 pair box hinges
6" silver or brass box chain
Optional: 4 small round brass box feet

Tools:

Basic Tools & Supplies (See list on page 41.)
Glass strip cutter
Needlenose pliers

Step-by-Step

Cut & Assemble:
See "General Instructions for Making Boxes" before you start to cut.

1. Square up your piece of glass so all four corners are 90-degree angles. Make sure the edges are smooth and straight.
2. Mark the grain of the glass with a felt-tip marker.
3. Set your strip cutter for 2" strips. Cut one 2" x 6" strip of glass for the front of the box. Cut one 4" x 6" strip for the top. Reset your strip cutter and cut three 2" x 6" strips for the back and sides.
4. To make the shorter sides of the box, cut the side pieces (pieces labeled SA and SB in the General Instructions) to 4-1/4" long. You can use the strip cutter or cut them by hand.
5. Now you are ready to separate the four box side bottoms (pieces labeled FB, BB, SAB, and SBB in the General Instructions) from the box side tops (pieces labeled FT, BT, SAT, and SBT). Set your strip cutter for 1-3/4". Follow the layout and double check the grain markings on the glass before you cut.
6. To cut the box top to accommodate the triangular beveled piece, first cut the top piece in half lengthwise. Place the two pieces side by side on your work board. Place the triangular beveled piece on top, with the point of the triangle on the cut. Trace around the edges of the triangle on the glass. Cut each piece of glass along the traced line.
7. Lay out the cut pieces of glass as shown in the General Instructions. Use a grinder to smooth the edges and make adjustments. The edges of each glass piece must be smooth and straight.

Apply Foil & Solder:
1. Wrap all the side bottom pieces and side top pieces in 7/32" copper foil.
2. Following the General Instructions, assemble the side top pieces and side bottom pieces of the box and tack-solder.
3. Wrap the three pieces of the top with copper foil and solder. Make sure the top fits easily inside the top sides.
4. Run a smooth solder bead over all inside copper seams. (You do not need to solder the outside edges now.) Turn the lid over and solder the back (the inside of the box lid).
5. To assemble the bottom of the box, wrap the mirror piece in foil and place flat on the work surface, mirror side up. Place the bottom side section around the mirror. The mirror should fit easily in the box. Tack-solder the corners of the mirror to the corners

continued on page 108

continued from page 107

of the box. Turn the box over and run a flat, smooth solder seam around the bottom edges, then solder the seams inside the box bottom.

Add Hinges:

1. Fit the top and bottom of the box together. Make sure you are happy with the fit. Secure with two rubber bands to help hold them together while you solder the hinges.
2. Position the hinges on the back of the box. Hold the hinges in place with needlenose pliers. Using a cotton swab or small paintbrush, paint flux on the edge of the hinge. *Tip:* Don't use too much flux or the solder will run into your hinge and ruin it. Remember solder can't travel where there is no flux.

Finish:

1. Solder the front and back outside seams of the box.
2. Solder a length of box chain inside the box to keep the lid from falling backward when opened.
3. *Optional:* Turn the box over and solder the four brass box feet in place.
4. Clean the project with soap and water. ❖

Confetti Glass Frame

This project is so easy you don't need a pattern. You can cut the pieces with a strip cutter or by hand using a ruler. This frame will accommodate a 4 x 6 photo, but you can alter the size to fit any photo.

Supplies

Glass:
Confetti, 5" x 7"
2 triangular clear beveled pieces, 3" x 3"
Clear, 4" x 6"

Other Supplies:
7/32" copper foil tape with silver backing
60/40 solder
Flux
18" piece of 1/8" zinc U-shaped came
Thin cardboard, size of photo

Tools:

Basic Tools & Supplies (See list on page 41.)
Came notcher

Step-by-Step

Cut & Assemble:

1. From confetti glass, cut two pieces 1" x 5" and two pieces each 1" x 7".
2. Using the photo as a guide, lay out the cut pieces of glass. Use a grinder to smooth edges and make adjustments.

Apply Foil & Solder:

1. Wrap each piece of glass and the two triangular beveled pieces in 7/32" copper foil.
2. Place pieces on work surface and secure, using push pins and wooden strips.
3. Tack-solder pieces in place.
4. Run a smooth solder bead over all inside copper seams. Solder the outside edges.
5. Turn project over. Solder the back of the frame. Do not build up a rounded bead like you did on the front.

Finish:

1. Using the came notcher or lead nippers, measure and cut 1/8" U-shaped zinc came to fit around the two sides and bottom of the clear glass piece. Tape the zinc came in place. Solder at the corners to secure it to the frame.
2. To make the stand, secure the frame upright with blocks of wood or coffee cans filled with sand. Position a beveled piece perpendicular to the side of the frame and solder it in place. Repeat on the other side using the other beveled piece.
3. Clean the project with soap and water.
4. Cut a piece of cardboard to use as a backing for your photo. ❖

Water Lily Box

You can create all kinds of beautiful floral boxes by simply varying the leaf shape, cutting out different-shaped flower petals, and arranging them. The pieces for the bottom can be wrapped with zinc came or copper foil.

The instructions for cutting the bottom of the box are written for using a strip cutter to cut the glass. If you are not using a strip cutter, use a ruler and your hand cutter.

Size: 5" x 9"

Supplies

Glass:
Blue rippled iridized, 6" x 6" (for sides of box bottom)
Green opalescent, 10" x 10" (for lily pad)
Pink opalescent, 8" x 8" (for flower)
Mirror, 1/8" thick, 6" x 3" (for inside of bottom)

Other Supplies:
6 ft. 1/8" U-shaped zinc came
3/16" copper foil tape
60/40 solder
Flux
1 pair box hinges
Black patina finish
Copper patina finish

Tools:

Basic Tools & Supplies (See list on page 41.)
Glass strip cutter
Came notcher

Continued on page 112.

Continued from page 110.

Step-by-Step

Cut the Bottom Pieces:
See "General Instructions for Making Boxes" before you begin to cut.
1. Square up your piece of glass so all four corners are 90-degree angles. Make sure the edges are smooth and straight.
2. Cut two strips 5-1/2" x 1-1/2" for the front and back of the box and two strips 3" x 1-1/2" for the sides of the box.

Prepare & Cut the Top:
1. Make two copies of the pattern for the top. Number and color-code each piece. Using pattern shears, cut out design from one copy.
2. Adhere pattern pieces to the glass and cut out the eight pieces that make up the flat part of the top plus five large, seven medium, and three small flower petals.
3. Grind the edges of each piece of glass as needed to fit the pattern. Clean all glass edges.
4. On your work board, tape or pin down the second copy of the pattern. Lay out the cut pieces of glass. Use the grinder to smooth edges and make adjustments. Each glass piece must fit within the pattern lines.

Apply Foil to Top Pieces & Solder:
1. Wrap each piece of glass for the top in 3/16" copper foil.
2. Pin the eight pieces that make up the flat part of the top in place, using push pins. Tack-solder together. Reserve the remaining flower petals.
3. Run a smooth solder bead over all copper seams. Turn top over and solder the back.

Attaching the water lily petals.

Apply Came & Solder Box Bottom:
1. Measure and notch the zinc came to fit around the four pieces of the bottom of the box. Wrap came around the glass pieces.
2. Solder each piece of came where the ends meet. (You now have four box sides framed in zinc came.)
3. Assemble the bottom of the box according to Fig. 1. Tack-solder the pieces together.
4. Check to see that the mirror fits easily inside the bottom of the box. Remove the mirror, wrap with zinc came, place it back inside the box bottom, and solder in place.

Attach Hinges:
1. Place the box top on the box bottom. Mark the location for the hinges on the back of the box and under the top as shown on pattern. Remove the box top and lay it face down on the work-table.
2. Position the hinges on the marks on the inside of the box top. Hold the hinges in place with needlenose pliers. Using a cotton swab or small brush, paint flux on the edge of the hinge. *Tip:* Don't use too much flux or the solder will run into your hinge

and ruin it. Remember solder can't travel where there is no flux.
3. Put the box top back on the box bottom. Double check the hinge location. Use two rubber bands to hold the top and bottom together. Solder the hinges in place on the bottom. Remove rubber bands.

Attach the Flower:
1. Brush the edges of the remaining foil-wrapped flower petals with flux and coat with solder.
2. Arrange the five large foil-wrapped petals on top of the box in the shape of a water lily. See photo. Tack-solder the spots that touch the foil seams on the top of the box. Secure with additional solder in the center of the petals. Add medium and small petals, one at a time.
3. To create the center of the water lily, cut small pieces of foil tape. Tin the tape by brushing with flux and coating with a thin layer of solder. Tack-solder them in place.
4. Clean the project with soap and water. Dry completely.
5. Apply black patina to the foil seams and copper patina to the zinc came, following manufacturer's instructions. (Copper patina turns zinc came black.) ❖

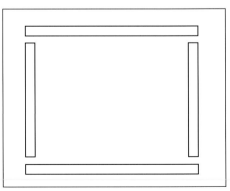
Fig. 1 - Box bottom assembly.

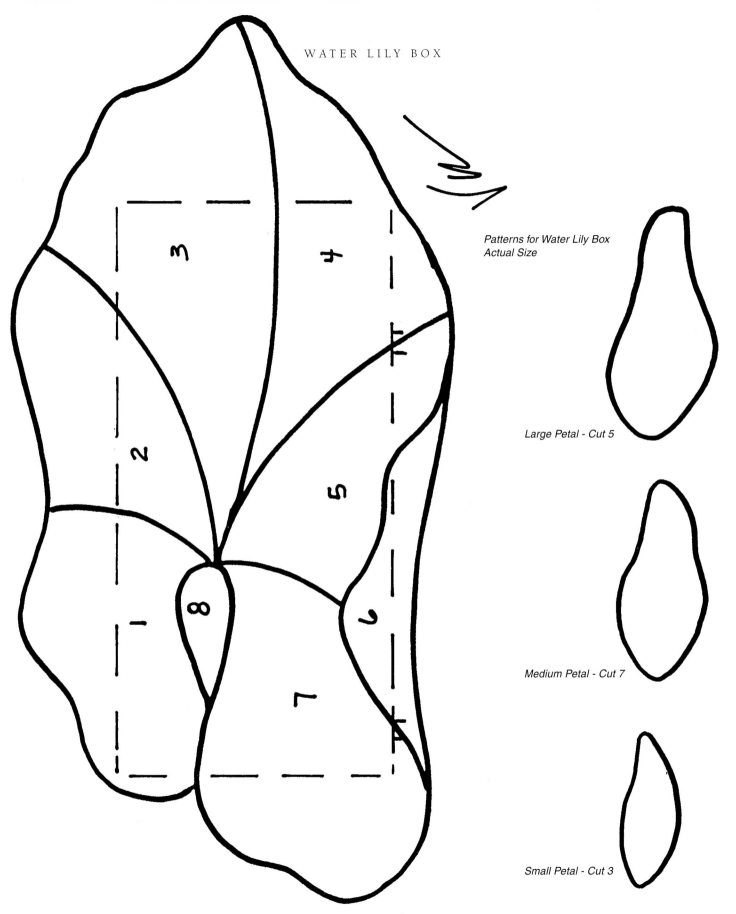

WATER LILY BOX

Patterns for Water Lily Box
Actual Size

Large Petal - Cut 5

Medium Petal - Cut 7

Small Petal - Cut 3

Box of Drawers

This drawer design is a box with two boxes that fit inside it. The decorative back panel is a separate piece that is soldered on the back of the assembled box. A pattern is provided for the back panel. All other pieces can be cut with a strip cutter.

Size: 4-1/4" deep x 7-1/4" tall x 4-1/4" wide

Supplies

Glass:
Blue opalescent, 16" x 16"
Green opalescent, 3" x 3"
Yellow opalescent, 3" x 3"

Other Supplies:
3/16" copper foil tape
4 round brass balls, 3/16" (for feet)
2 round brass balls, 1/4" diameter (for drawer pulls)
60/40 solder
Flux
Black patina finish

Tools:
Basic Tools & Supplies (See list on page 41.)
Glass strip cutter

Step-by-Step

Prepare, Cut & Assemble the Back Panel:
1. Make two copies of the pattern. Number and color-code each piece. Adhere pattern pieces to the glass. Cut out each piece.
2. Grind the edges of each piece as needed to fit the pattern. Clean all glass edges.
3. On your work board, tape or pin down the second copy of the pattern. Lay out the cut pieces of glass. Use the grinder to smooth edges and make adjustments. Each glass piece must fit within the pattern lines.

Apply Foil to Back Panel & Solder:
1. Wrap each piece of glass for the back panel in 3/16" copper foil.
2. Pin pieces in place on pattern, using push pins.
3. Tack-solder pieces in place.
4. Run a smooth solder bead over all inside copper seams. Keep the seams flat around the edges of the project so the side pieces will fit smoothly against the back.

5. Turn the panel over and solder the back.

Cut the Box & Drawers:
To get the best use of your glass, plan before you start to cut.

Make sure your glass is completely square and all the edges are straight. Cut these pieces:

For the box:
2 pieces, each 4-1/4" x 4" (box top and bottom)
2 pieces, each 4" x 4" (box sides)
1 piece, 3-7/8" x 4" (divider shelf)
For the drawers:
4 pieces, each 1-3/4" x 3-3/4" (sides)
4 pieces, each 1-3/4" x 3-7/8" (fronts and backs)
2 pieces, each 3-3/4" x 3-5/8" (bottoms)

Assemble the Box & Drawers:
1. Use the grinder as necessary to smooth edges of glass. Check to be sure each piece is square and the edges are straight.
2. Wrap each piece of glass in 3/16" copper foil.

continued on page 116

continued from page 117

3. Assemble box according to Fig. 1. Tack-solder pieces.

4. Assemble drawers according to Fig. 2. Talk-solder pieces.

5. Place the divider shelf 2" from the top of the box. Tack-solder in place at the front of the box and at both back corners.

6. Check box and drawers for fit. Make adjustments as needed so drawers slide in and out smoothly. When you are happy with the fit, solder all copper edges. Keep the solder smooth and flat—lumpy solder will interfere with the fit.

7. Solder feet to the four corners of the bottom of the box.

8. Solder drawer pulls to drawer fronts.

Finish:

1. Position back panel on the back of the box and solder the seams at the sides and bottom.

2. Clean project with soap and water.

3. Apply patina according to manu-facturer's instructions. ❖

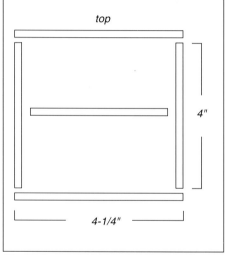

Fig. 1 - Box Assembly

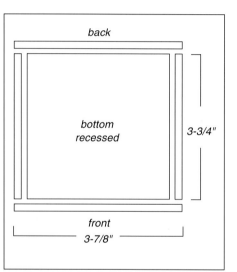

Fig. 2 - Drawer Assembly

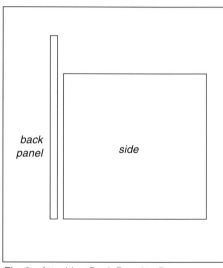

Fig. 3 - Attaching Back Panel to Box

*Pattern for Box of Drawers
Actual size*

How to Create Glass Mosaics

Finished mosaics may look complicated, but mosaic techniques are easy to learn and many mosaic projects are quick and simple to do. Although the most common mosaic material today is tile, many early mosaics were made of glass. The mosaic projects in this book are created by cutting design motifs from glass using the patterns provided. The cut-out motifs are glued on a surface and the areas around the motifs are filled in with randomly placed small pieces of glass. The piece is then grouted — an easy process.

Making a mosaic is a great way to use small scraps of glass left over from other projects. No soldering is required.

To create glass mosaics, you need:

- **Opalescent glass**, the same type of art glass used for many of the other projects in this book.
- **A surface**, to use as a base, such as wood or terra cotta.
- **An adhesive**, such as white craft glue or silicone adhesive, to hold the glass to the surface.
- **Sanded grout**, to fill the spaces between the pieces of glass, to create a smooth surface, and to add strength and durability.
- **Grout sealer**, to seal the grout and protect it.
- **Tools**, including the same glass cutting tools you've used for other projects in this book, plus **glass nippers** (sometimes called "mosaic cutters") for breaking the small background pieces, some **craft sticks** for applying the adhesive, a **putty knife or spatula or stiff-bristled brush** for applying grout, a **sponge** for wiping grout, and some **soft cloth rags** for polishing.
- **Safety gear**, such as a dust mask and rubber gloves for working with grout, plus safety glasses for cutting glass.

The Mosaic Technique

1. **Cut Glass Pieces:** Cut glass pattern pieces the same as you would for a regular stained glass project.
2. **Glue.** Apply glue to the back of the glass pattern pieces. Place cut glass pieces on the surface. Let dry completely. *If you are not sure of placing the pattern pieces on the glass surface, you can transfer the pattern to the surface with transfer paper. Then arrange the cut pieces onto the transferred pattern outline.*
3. **Fill in Background:** Using nippers break small pieces of glass to fill in background. Glue these in place.
4. **Grout.** Mix grout according to manufacturer's instructions. Use a stiff-bristle brush, a putty knife or a spatula to apply the grout, pressing it into the spaces between the glass pieces.
5. **Wipe.** Fill a bowl with water. Dampen a sponge and squeeze out excess water. Wipe the piece to remove excess grout from the surface of the glass pieces. Rinse the sponge and wipe again. Repeat until you can see all the pieces though the grout and the grout is smooth and even with the surface of the glass. Let dry.
6. **Polish.** As the grout dries, a haze will form over the glass. Polish off the haze by rubbing with a soft cloth rag until the glass gleams. ❖

Rose Box

Pictured on page 119.

The stylized rose-and-leaf design is used on the top of the box and, in a smaller version, on the three sides. The spaces around the design are filled with randomly placed irregular pieces of black glass.

You can decorate the inside of the box with paint, fabric, or paper. It's a good idea to attach some self-adhesive felt pads or glue a piece of felt on the bottom to protect tabletops.

Supplies

Glass:
Opalescent black, 1/2 sq. ft. (for background)
Opalescent pink, 1/2 sq. ft. (for rose)
Opalescent lime green, 1/2 sq. ft. (for leaves)
Opalescent dark green, 1/2 sq. ft. (for leaves)

Other Supplies:
Triangular 7" unfinished wooden box
Adhesive
Gray grout
Grout sealer
8" cording or ribbon
Transfer paper & stylus

Tools:
Basic Tools & Supplies (See list on page 41.)
Mosaic Tools (See "How to Create Glass Mosaics.")

Step-by-Step

Prepare & Cut Design:
1. Make two copies of the pattern for the top and four copies of the pattern for the sides. Number and color-code one copy for the top and three copies for the sides. Using pattern shears, cut out design from the color-coded copies.
2. Adhere pattern pieces to the glass. Cut out each piece.
3. Grind the edges of each piece as needed to fit the pattern. Clean all glass edges.
4. Mark the centers of the box top and sides. Tape the other copy of the patterns to the box and transfer the design to the box surface, using transfer paper and a stylus.

Glue Pieces & Cut Background:
1. Adhere cut glass pieces over the transferred pattern on the box top and sides.
2. Cut an elliptical shaped piece to use as a handle. Use the glass grinder to smooth the edges. Glue the handle at the front point of the box, allowing it to extend 1/2" beyond the box top.
3. Using glass nippers, cut small triangular pieces (about 3/8") of black glass to fill in the spaces around the design on the top and sides.
4. Glue the background pieces in place around the rose design, leaving at least 1/8" around the edge of the box to allow for grout. Let dry.

Grout:
See "The Mosaic Technique." Close the box and keep it closed throughout the grouting process.
1. Mix grout according to manufacturer's instructions.
2. Apply grout over the top and sides of the box, across the opening and over the hinges. Clean off excess with a damp sponge.
3. Keeping the box closed, use a craft stick to remove grout from the hinges and the back box opening. Open the box—you should have smooth, clean edges around the opening. Let dry completely.

Finish:
1. Apply grout sealer according to the manufacturer's instructions. Let dry.
2. Glue a piece of ribbon inside the box to keep the lid from falling backward when opened. ❖

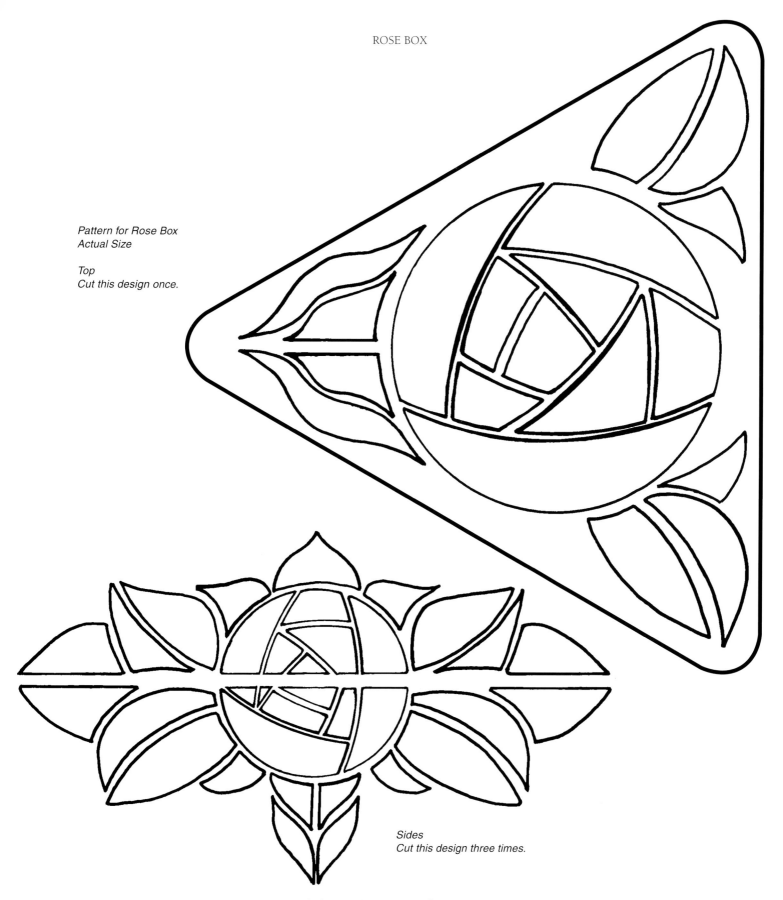

Pattern for Rose Box
Actual Size

Top
Cut this design once.

Sides
Cut this design three times.

Dragonfly Box

This Arts-and-Crafts-inspired box has a dragonfly motif on the top and waterlilies on the sides.

Supplies

Glass:
Opalescent black, 1/2 sq. ft. (for background of sides)

Opalescent pink, 1/2 sq. ft. (for background of top and flowers)

Opalescent lime green, 1/2 sq. ft. (for wings and flower stems)

Opalescent dark green, 1/2 sq. ft. (for dragonfly body)

Other Supplies:
Triangular 7" unfinished wooden box

Adhesive

Gray grout

Grout sealer

8" cording or ribbon

Transfer paper & stylus

Tools:
Basic Tools & Supplies (See list on page 41.)

Mosaic Tools (See "How to Create Glass Mosaics.")

Step-by-Step

Prepare & Cut Design:
1. Make two copies of the pattern for the top and four copies of the pattern for the sides. Number and color-code one copy for the top and three copies for the sides. Using pattern shears, cut out design from the color-coded copies.
2. Adhere pattern pieces to the glass. Cut out each piece.
3. Grind the edges of each piece as needed to fit the pattern. Clean all glass edges.
4. Position the other copy of the patterns to the box and transfer the design, using transfer paper and a stylus.

Glue Pieces & Cut Background:
1. Adhere cut glass pieces over the transferred pattern on the box top and sides.
2. Cut an elliptical shaped piece to use as a handle. Use the glass grinder to smooth the edges. Glue the handle at the front point of the box, allowing it to extend 1/2" beyond the box top.
3. Using glass nippers, cut small triangular pieces (about 3/8") of black glass to fill in the spaces around the design on the sides.

4. Glue the background pieces in place on the sides, leaving at least 1/8" around the edge of the box to allow for grout. Let dry.

Grout:
See "The Mosaic Technique." Close the box and keep it closed throughout the grouting process.
1. Mix grout according to manufacturer's instructions.
2. Apply grout over the top and sides of the box, across the opening and over the hinges. Clean off excess with a damp sponge.
3. Keeping the box closed, use a craft stick to remove grout from the hinges and the back box opening. Open the box—you should have smooth, clean edges around the opening. Let dry completely.

Finish:
1. Apply grout sealer according to the manufacturer's instructions. Let dry.
2. Glue a piece of ribbon inside the box to keep the lid from falling backward when opened. ❖

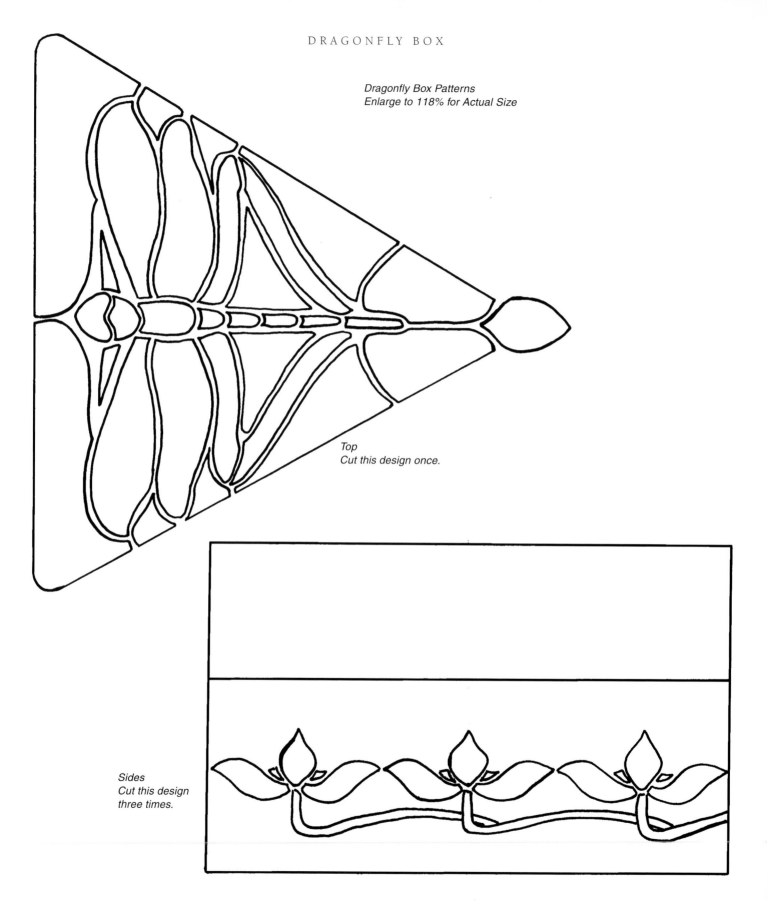

Dragonfly Box Patterns
Enlarge to 118% for Actual Size

Top
Cut this design once.

Sides
Cut this design
three times.

Rose Bird Baths
Instructions on page 126

Rose Bird Baths

Pictured on page 125

The bowls for these bird baths are made from terra cotta saucers; the stands are terra cotta pots turned upside down. They are especially quick and easy to make if you use pre-cut rose and leaf motifs, which often can be purchased at crafts and hobby stores where stained glass supplies are sold. You can, of course, cut your own rose and leaf motifs, using the patterns supplied.

The patina faux finish on the terra cotta is created with acrylic craft paint.

Supplies

Glass:
For the large bird bath:
3 red glass rose motifs
10-12 green glass leaf motifs
30" green glass stems, nipped into pieces 1/2" long
Yellow opalescent glass, 1 sq. ft.

For the small bird bath:
1 red glass rose motif
3 green glass leaf motifs
Yellow opalescent glass, 1 sq. ft.

Other Supplies:
Adhesive
Gray grout
Grout sealer
Transfer paper & stylus
Acrylic craft paint - gray, light green
For large birdbath: Terra cotta saucer, 14" diameter and terra cotta pot
For small bird bath: Terra cotta saucer, 12" diameter and terra cotta pot

Tools:

Basic Tools & Supplies (See list on page 41.)
Mosaic Tools (See "How to Create Glass Mosaics.")
Cellulose sponge

Step-by-Step

Prepare & Cut Design:
If you are cutting your own glass:
1. Make two copies of the pattern. Number and color-code one copy. Using pattern shears, cut out design from the color-coded copy.
2. Adhere pattern pieces to the glass. Cut out each piece.
3. Grind the edges of each piece as needed to fit the pattern. Clean all glass edges.
4. Position the other copy of the pattern on the saucer and transfer the design, using transfer paper and a stylus.

If you are using pre-cut glass motifs:
Copy pattern. Position on saucer and transfer the design, using transfer paper and a stylus.

Glue Motifs & Cut Background:
1. Adhere cut glass pieces *or* pre-cut motifs over the transferred pattern.
2. Using glass nippers, cut pieces of yellow glass to fill in the spaces around the rose motif(s). Let dry.

Grout:
See "The Mosaic Technique."
1. Mix grout according to manufacturer's instructions.
2. Apply grout over the bottom of the saucer. Clean off excess with a damp sponge. Let dry completely.

Finish:
1. Apply grout sealer according to the manufacturer's instructions. Let dry.
2. Dampen sponge. Sponge edges and bottom of saucer(s) and outside(s) of terra cotta pot(s) with gray paint, then with light green paint, to create a patina faux finish. Let dry.
3. Place saucer(s) on pot(s) as shown in photo. ❖

Pattern for Rose Bird Bath
Actual Size Pattern
Repeat rose pattern for large saucer with three roses

Metric Conversion Chart

Inches to Millimeters and Centimeters

Inches	MM	CM	Inches	MM	CM
1/8	3	.3	2	51	5.1
1/4	6	.6	3	76	7.6
3/8	10	1.0	4	102	10.2
1/2	13	1.3	5	127	12.7
5/8	16	1.6	6	152	15.2
3/4	19	1.9	7	178	17.8
7/8	22	2.2	8	203	20.3
1	25	2.5	9	229	22.9
1-1/4	32	3.2	10	254	25.4
1-1/2	38	3.8	11	279	27.9
1-3/4	44	4.4	12	305	30.5

Yards to Meters

Yards	Meters	Yards	Meters
1/8	.11	3	2.74
1/4	.23	4	3.66
3/8	.34	5	4.57
1/2	.46	6	5.49
5/8	.57	7	6.40
3/4	.69	8	7.32
7/8	.80	9	8.23
1	.91	10	9.14
2	1.83		

Index